Grave Anatomy:

101 Uses for a Dead Human Body

A Nonfiction Book by

Tony Wilson

Illustrations by

Alex Reece

Table of Contents

No dead human bodies were harmed in the making of this book.

Introduction

"We are stardust,

Billion year old carbon"

Joni Mitchell,

"Woodstock," 1970

Joni Mitchell was right. Human beings are made of carbon, one of the most common elements in the universe and the basic building block of nature found in every life form.

The human body is also made of silicon, the second most abundant element in the earth's crust, used to construct things as diverse as microchips and breast implants. And just as two-thirds of our planet's surface is covered in water, our bodies are two-thirds H_2O.

We're also a little bit uranium, but just a little bit. It takes a lot to make an atom bomb.

The human body is made up of a lot of things, and a lot of things could be made out of a human body. Early scientists knew this when they dissected human cadavers for medical research, and ancient warmongers who used infected corpses to spread disease to an opposing army. But the human body also contains dozens of distinct elements, some in microscopic amounts. These elements could be used in limitless ways, if there was a way to harvest them.

We ingest herbal remedies, take vitamins and

receive organ transplants to prolong our lives. It's no surprise that a human cadaver can provide replacement organs, but dead human bodies have also been used to create herbal powders, and could supply the active ingredients in many vitamin supplements.

What follows is a collection of applications--some real, some not-so-much--based on the actual contents of the human body. You'll be surprised to discover just how many elements define who we are, so to speak.

Just as each of us has found a place in this world, the world and its many elements have found a place in each of us. So consider this book a user's guide to the planet's greatest natural resource…you.

Chapter One
Cosmetic and Optical Procedures

It's possible to look better dead than alive, thanks to modern science and the degree some people will go to satisfy their vanity. Funeral directors practice restorative art, a term commonly applied to embalming and the cosmetic procedures undertaken to make deceased people, often ravaged by age and disease, look the way they did during healthier and happier times.

But as our beauty-obsessed society confronts its mortality, some people go further than a little touch-up. "A funeral is their last major event and they want to look good for it," said Everest Funeral president and CEO Mark Duffey in a 2008 MSNBC report. "I've even had people say, 'I want you to get rid of my wrinkles and make me look younger.'" Added funeral director David Temrowski, "I've had people mention that they want their breasts to look perky when they're dead."

The best of both worlds is to look good while you're still alive, perhaps with a little assist from the dead. As the following uses detail, the human body is a reservoir of constructive materials, some of which really have been used to make the living look drop dead gorgeous.

Making Mountains out of Molehills
Use #1: Saline Breast Implants

The world is expanding, in more ways than one. Economies and deficits grow, the population increases and, in a development likely to make teenage boys cheer, the average bra size has swelled, too.

Bust sizes vary between different regions, likely affected by lifestyle choices such as diet. According to manufacturers, the average American bra size has increased over the years from 34B to 36C, with 34 and 36 referring to the circumference of a bra in inches and B and C referring to the cup size.

But if diet and nature don't provide someone with the desired attributes, medical science has found time in between curing diseases and treating illnesses to enhance the female form. In a nutshell, the size of a woman's bust is adjustable, specifically through the use of saline breast implants.

Saline is a sterile solution of sodium chloride (salt) and water. The human body contains all of the necessary elements to make a saline solution, though saline composition differs depending on how it is used. If we assume a common medical saline composition of 0.9% sodium chloride, one human body could produce about 17.4 liters of saline.

That's over four and a half gallons of implant-worthy saline, and could provide the saline content for about 145 small (120 cc) breast implants. But rarely do the mammary-challenged opt for small implants, so the saline from one dead human body could also provide the saline content for 22 large (800 cc) breast implants. That's 11 pairs of DD breasts, just one pair shy of a Playboy calendar.

Through the Looking Glasses
Use #2: Corrective Lenses

Corrective glasses improve the vision of nearsighted, farsighted, and astigmatic people by employing eyeglass lenses with varying refractive qualities. The refractive index is affected by the curve of the lens and the materials used to make the lens, such as glass, plastic and various metals.

Niobium pentoxide is a niobium/oxygen compound used to make corrective lenses; 1.75 milligrams of niobium pentoxide could be fashioned from one dead human body. The weight of an eyeglass lens depends on many variables, such as the type of materials used to make it, the nature of the eye disorder, and the style of eyeglass frames.

If we assume an eyeglass lens weight of 4 grams, and the amount of niobium pentoxide used as 30% of the total weight of the lens, then the niobium pentoxide from about 686 dead human bodies could provide the needed amount for one lens. But what good is one lens, except for wearing a monocle? Unless you want to look like Mr. Peanut, you'd better mine the niobium pentoxide content of an additional 686 dead donors to make a second lens.

Eyeglass Facts

English philosopher Roger Bacon documented the optical use of a lens in 1268, around the same time Marco Polo chronicled the use of eyeglasses in China, while other stories credit Italian inventor Salvino D'Armate with the invention in 1284.

Eyeglasses are depicted in numerous paintings dating from the Middle Ages. Demand for eyeglasses grew during the 15th century after the invention of the printing press. Maybe that's why they were called the Dark Ages.

Framed
Use #3. Eyeglass Frames

Now that you've fixed your vision with corrective lenses, it's time to pick eyeglass frames.

Frames can be made from a variety of materials, including plastics, wood, precious stones, and a variety of metals or metal mixtures. Eyeglass frames can also be made out of bone.

An adult person's skeleton accounts for about 20% of a person's weight, so the bones from one dead human body could produce 1,750 pairs of eyeglass frames, each weighing about eight grams. The human bone frames won't be as flexible as other materials, but imagine shooting your enemies the look of death…literally.

If That's Not Bone-Chilling Enough…

One dead human body contains 20 milligrams of titanium, a popular, flexible and durable metal used to make eyeglass frames.

If you spring for 100% pure titanium frames, you'd need the titanium content of 400 dead human bodies to make one pair. Sound excessive? Just look the other way, which will be easy to do with your new glasses.

Looks to Die For
Use #4: Collagen Injections

Collagen is a common protein found throughout the human body, an important substance in the production of connective tissues like ligaments and tendons. It also strengthens and improves skin flexibility and aids in the creation of bones. When skin is damaged by an injury, a critical part of the healing process is the formation of new collagen to repair the wound.

The healing power of collagen has not been lost on the medical and cosmetic industries. Collagen can be used to make artificial heart valves, cosmetics and hair care products, in addition to glues and certain types of food. Most of the collagen used to manufacture these products is taken from dead animals.

Dead human bodies would seem an unlikely source for collagen used in the cosmetics industry, but in 2005 a cosmetics company in China was discovered harvesting collagen from the skin of executed criminals for use in beauty supply products sold throughout Europe.

Far from denying this allegation, representatives from the cosmetics company told undercover agents posing as clients that the practice is commonplace and, in the words of one representative, nothing “to make such a big fuss about.” Aside from the squirm factor, harvesting collagen from dead human bodies poses serious ethical and hygienic problems.

Popular collagen procedures include facial injections that enhance the size and shape of lips and reduce wrinkles. But collagen improperly harvested and not tested for harmful byproducts can cause infections and skin inflammations, which in turn can lead to permanent discomfort, scarring and severe disfigurement.

The Chinese cosmetics company later released a statement officially denying using executed prisoners to manufacture cosmetic collagen products, but European governments have since moved to create new regulations to inspect and restrict collagen imports. Beauty may be skin deep, but the depths some people will go to achieve beauty can cut too deep.

Dead Body Harvesting

Rumors persist that China also uses materials from executed prisoners for organ and hand transplants. One anecdote describes a doctor removing skin from a recently executed criminal whose heart was still beating in order to treat a burn victim.

Chapter Two
Health Remedies

Rolling Stones guitarist Keith Richards isn't bashful about his drug use, but this disclosure in a 2007 issue of NME Magazine rocked even his most callous fans: "The strangest thing I've tried to snort? My father. I snorted my father….He was cremated and I couldn't resist grinding him up with a little bit of blow. My dad wouldn't have cared." But a lot of people did, prompting Richards to issue a denial claiming that he was only joking.

Whether he did or not, human cremation is unlike anything found in your medicine cabinet--unless you've ever purchased mummy powder or cured an ailment using any of the following remedies.

My Mummy's an Apothecary

Use #5: Egyptian Mummy Powder

Mummification was practiced in Ancient Egypt for thousands of years, though the custom was long out of fashion by the time European crusaders plundered Egyptian tombs for treasure, artifacts, and the bodies themselves.

The Europeans discovered a tar-like substance similar to bitumen inside the mummies. Bitumen was believed to have healing powers, so the bitumen-like stuff that filled the skull, chest and abdominal cavities of the mummies was thought to have healing powers, too. European traders extracted this material and marketed the substance as a medicinal cure, but removing the brittle material proved tricky, so later traders simply sliced up the mummies and grinded them down into a fine powder.

Mummy powder can be used both internally and externally, though you should consult your doctor before taking any new medications. Of course, if your doctor recommends anything other than discarding the mummy powder, you should probably find a new doctor.

You Could Be a Mummy, Too

If spending eternity wrapped up in fine linen sounds like a gas, then the ancient art of mummification might be right for you. Similar to modern embalming, mummification was perfected over a period of thousands of years and practiced mainly by wealthy Egyptians who could afford the materials. Modern mummy makers will find the going rate a little more reasonable.

First, your dead body will be washed in natron salt dissolved in water, overseen by priests and assistants. Your internal organs, save your heart, will be extracted through an incision in your abdomen and placed in their own jars, because you'll need them in the afterlife. Your brain, which was not highly regarded in Egyptian culture, will be removed by a long, thin-hooked instrument inserted through your nose. The instrument will break through your ethmoid bone and into your cranium, where the hook will splice up your brain like a food processor and remove your skull's contents. Imagine pulling Top Ramen from a bottleneck and you'll get the idea.

Your body will next spend 40 days packed in natron salt, which removes any remaining moisture and prepares your body for the stuffing. After an oil rubdown, your empty carcass is filled with a number of materials, including sawdust, rags used during your preparation, and other rubbish that happens to be lying around. Your eyeballs, which have sunk deep into your eye sockets, will be replaced by elaborate jewels or fine stones. If you can't afford that, onion bulbs will do.

The priest and his assistants will spend the next two weeks wrapping your body in precious linens, which every Egyptian spent a lifetime collecting. You, on the other hand, can head to the nearest retail store and buy some common bed sheets (you'll be wrapped up for eternity, so why not splurge on a high thread count?).

You'll need a few hundred yards of linen, plus any jewelry you'd like to be buried with, since vanity is as important in death as it was in life.

The wrapping will take awhile. Egyptians followed a strict, careful method to protect your frail cadaver, which is now much lighter minus its water content. If you're lucky, wild animals will not sneak into your embalming tent at night and make off with a salty snack courtesy of your appendages.

Finally, your bandaged body will be tightly wrapped in burial shrouds and escorted to your burial sight, where hired grievers will weep in your honor and skilled craftsmen have prepared your casket. You'll be loaded into a stone sarcophagus, surrounded by your worldly possessions (which will come in useful in the afterlife, where hunger and desire continue unabated). After the ceremonial weighing of your heart (a purely symbolic gesture, since your ticker is still in place), your tomb is now ready to be sealed…and later plundered by any manner of scavengers, treasure hunters or, if you're lucky, intrepid archaeologists.

So, after all that work, your best hope for everlasting posterity is to serve as an exhibit in a museum…or maybe a prop in a horror movie. That's a wrap.

Mummy Facts

Bitumen, the tar-like substance found inside Egyptian mummies, was also known as moumia, which inspired the name "mummy."

Mining a mummy for medicine dates back to the middle ages, though the practice continued as recently as the early 20th century. The sales list of a German company in 1924 offered "Mumia vera Aegyptica," for the price of 12 gold marks per kilo.

All the Poop on Laxatives
Use #6: Epsom Salt

If Dr. Luigi Capasso is right, one of the earliest known laxatives was used 5,300 years ago by some prehistoric guy with a tummy ache.

Dr. Capasso asserts that the Iceman, whose mummified remains were discovered in Italy in 1991, carried with him a fungus, Piptoporus betulinus, that attacked the parasites in his stomach and purged his intestines. Tree fungus is a far cry from Ex-Lax, but the Iceman had the right idea.

Modern day laxatives can be eaten, swallowed as a pill or liquid, or inserted rectally by means of an enema. Some laxatives, like mineral oil, lubricate the bowel contents, while Epsom salt forces the contents out by increasing the amount of water in the bowels. Natural remedies like drinking a lot of water and eating fiber-rich foods should always be tried first since long-term laxative use can weaken bowel functions.

Flushing Out the Facts

Magnesium sulfate, also known as Epsom salt, is a potent laxative. The elements needed to make magnesium sulfate (magnesium, sulfur, and oxygen) can be found in the human body.

One dead human body could produce about 56 grams (1.9 oz) of magnesium sulfate. Magnesium sulfate requires water to become Epsom salt (magnesium sulfate heptahydrate), which the human body also contains. The dosage directions on a box of Epsom salt recommend two to six level teaspoons daily (10 to 30 grams) mixed with a glass of water to treat constipation.

If a constipation sufferer took the maximum recommended dosage, one dead human body could produce two doses of Epsom salt. If the average person produces about two pounds of feces a day, then the Epsom salt from one dead human body could help purge almost four pounds of feces.

That's probably more information than you wanted to know, unless you're currently suffering from constipation, in which case the effectiveness of Epsom salt is the exact thing you wanted to know.

The Business of Bismuth
Use #7: Pepto-Bismol

Have you ever noticed a darkening of your stool after taking Pepto-Bismol (come on, you know you've looked)? The temporary darkening is caused by the active ingredient bismuth, which reacts with trace amounts of sulfur in your saliva and gastrointestinal tract. The resulting black substance is called bismuth sulfide, a harmless byproduct that normally subsides within a few days of stopping Pepto-Bismol treatment.

And if you think that's interesting, pepto-bismol.com has a wealth of information about the world-famous stomach soother. First developed to fight cholera infantum, a major cause of infant death up until the early 20th century, the pink liquid was once dispensed at drugstore soda fountains and is now available in many countries around the world.

In the Pink

Bismuth subsalicylate is the active ingredient in Pepto-Bismol that treats heartburn, diarrhea, and other stomach ailments. Bismuth, carbon, hydrogen, and oxygen are the elements that produce bismuth subsalicylate, and each are found in the human body. In fact, oxygen, carbon and hydrogen are the most common elements in the human body, though only 0.5 milligrams of bismuth is present. All four combined equal a modest 571 micrograms of bismuth subsalicylate.

You'd need the bismuth subsalicylate content of about 459 dead human bodies to make one tablespoon (15 ml) of Pepto-Bismol. The recommended dosage is two tablespoons, requiring the bismuth subsalicylate content of about 917 dead human bodies. A full days serving of Pepto-Bismol calls for the bismuth subsalicylate contents of about 7,339 dead human bodies. Kind of makes you queasy, huh?

Clear Your Throat

Use #8: Zinc Throat Lozenges

Experts are unsure what effect zinc lozenges have on a cold. Zinc does strengthen the immune system, while throat lozenges soothe irritated throats and suppress coughs. But most zinc lozenges contain other ingredients, like vitamin C, that also boost the immune system, and inconclusive test results cast further doubt on the effectiveness of zinc on a cold.

Nevertheless, if your runny nose demands treatment beyond chicken soup and a warm blankie, zinc lozenges are available in a variety of flavors and dosages, anywhere from five to 20 or more milligrams of zinc per lozenge. Some products advertise as much as 50 mg of zinc, although the recommended daily intake is only 15 mg.

If we assume a zinc content of five mg, one dead human body could provide the zinc content for 460 zinc lozenges. If a bag of 15 zinc lozenges costs $2.50, one dead human body could produce enough zinc for 30 bags with a retail value of $75.00.

If a cold sufferer took one zinc lozenge every two hours, one dead human body could produce enough zinc to keep that sicko sucking on lozenges for 38 days straight. That's much longer than the average cold lasts, and it's also more zinc than you should consume, since too much zinc over a long period of time can actually weaken your immune system.

If You Think Throat Lozenges Suck...

Zinc can also be consumed as a throat spray. If a bottle of zinc throat spray contains 100 doses, and each dose contains 10 mg of zinc, one dead human body could provide the zinc content for over two bottles of zinc throat spray, for a total of 230 doses. Hard to swallow, isn't it?

Treat Your Body Right

Use #9: Vitamin Supplements

Our doctors tell us to take vitamin supplements to ensure a long and healthy life. After we die, our bodies leave behind elements that could be used to make vitamin supplements.

Calcium is the most abundant mineral in the human body, to the tune of one kilogram. Almost all of our calcium is found in our bones, since calcium strengthens bones and helps prevent osteoporosis. Calcium also aids in muscle contraction, regulating the heartbeat, and blood clotting. Calcium supplements are available in 600 mg tablets, so one dead human body could provide the calcium for 1,666 tablets.

The human body contains 4.2 grams of iron. Iron is essential for transporting oxygen through the body--the important role of hemoglobin in red blood cells. Iron deficiency can lead to anemia, which is characterized by fatigue, lack of concentration, and increased susceptibility to infections. 65 mg iron tablets can help stave off iron-deficiency anemia. One dead human body could provide the iron for 64 tablets.

Zinc is also found in the human body, especially in the brain, liver, kidneys, and eyes. 30 mg zinc tablets help the immune system function properly, serve as an antioxidant and are an important part of a healthy pregnancy. The 2.3 grams of zinc in one dead human body could provide enough zinc for 76 tablets.

200 mcg selenium tablets bolster the immune system and support other antioxidant-stimulating vitamins. The modest 15 mg of selenium found in one dead human body could fortify 75 selenium tablets.

So, if your friends accuse you of living an unhealthy lifestyle, remind them that your body is actually chockfull of vitamins.

For Use With Minor Cuts and Bruises
Use #10: Iodine

Iodine is the scourge of all scourges for a ten year old with a knee scrape, the burning punishment doled out for recklessly riding a skateboard or climbing a brick wall. For parents, iodine is an important infection-fighting weapon.

Tincture of iodine is a common antiseptic sold in one-ounce bottles, usually containing 2% iodine and

2.4% sodium iodine. The human body contains 20 milligrams of iodine and 100 grams of sodium. When combined, one human body could produce 23.55 milligrams of sodium iodine.

The sodium and iodine from one dead human body could supply the sodium iodine content for one milliliter of tincture of iodine, while one additional dead human body could supply the iodine content. So children, if you don't treat your skinned knee with iodine you might die from an infection--then your corpse will be mined for its iodine content. Consider yourself warned.

Iodine Facts

First discovered in the early 18th century, iodine and its compounds are used in many industries including photography, baking, and medicine. If your own burning desire for all things iodine can't get enough, iodine has its own website: iodine.com.

Warts and All
Use #11: Wart Removal

Despite the old wives tale, you cannot catch warts by touching a toad. A wart is an infection, a benign tumor usually found on hands and feet that can be transmitted through person-to-person contact. So if you're best friend has warts, you're better off touching a toad. Unless your best friend happens to be a toad, in which case you should make new friends.

In the event that you contract a wart and do not wish to lose any friends, there are a variety of treatment options. A wart can be treated by a doctor using cryotherapy (liquid nitrogen, which freezes the wart), chemical treatments, or removal by surgery or laser. If left alone, some warts will disappear naturally.

The Big Chill

Liquid nitrogen applied by a medical professional is a quick and effective way to treat a wart. Better still, if your best friend happens to croak prior to your treatment, he could bequeath you the 1.8 kilograms of nitrogen in his dead body.

The nitrogen in the human body is in gaseous form, since liquid nitrogen must be cooled to an extremely chilly -321 degrees F (-196 degrees C). If your best friend is wealthy, ask him to leave you a small cash inheritance so you can buy a cryogenic delivery system to cool, store and dispense your liquid nitrogen, which will run you about $1500.00.

The 1.8 kilograms of nitrogen gas in the human body translates to a volume of approximately 1.43 kiloliters. Since nitrogen gas has about 700 times the volume of liquid nitrogen, the nitrogen content of one dead human body could produce about 2.04 liters of liquid nitrogen. That's almost half the capacity of a typical cryogenic dispenser, so unless you've spread your warts to all of your friends, you should be sufficiently stocked to treat your own infection.

Good to Know

Washing your hands regularly and avoiding towels used by a wart sufferer are the best ways to avoid contracting warts. A fresh wound is more likely to develop a wart, so soap and disinfectant are a must.

Wart Facts

Over-the-counter and home remedies include using salicylic acid for several weeks to gradually peel off the wart, applying duct tape for a couple of months to irritate the wart (prompting the body to heal it), or purchasing a take-home cryotherapy kit.

What appear to be warts on a toad are actually glands that emit a toxin if the toad is threatened. The glands differentiate toads from frogs, since frogs have smooth skin.

Chapter Three
Health and Beauty

"Live fast, die young and leave a beautiful corpse."

attributed to James Dean

If beauty is in the eye of the beholder, than the beholder must be a dead human body. Many of the elements used to manufacture health and beauty products are also found in the human body, some in quantities large enough to stock a medicine cabinet.

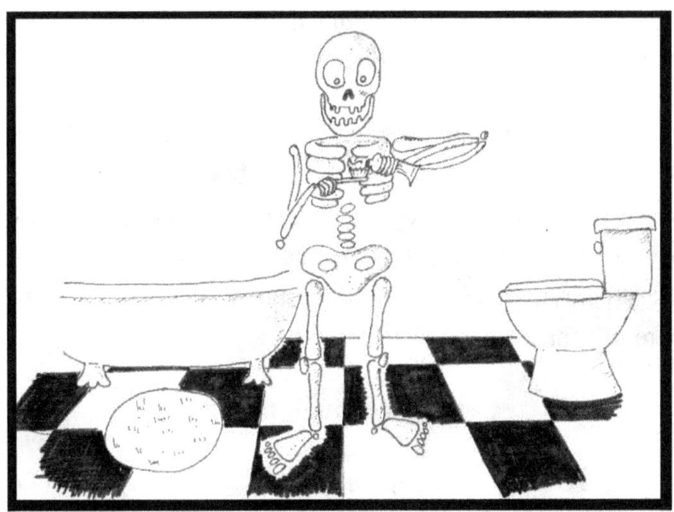

Dirty Business
Use #12: Soap

Chuck Palahniuk's novel *Fight Club* describes a character using liposuctioned body fat from a cosmetic surgery clinic to produce high-end soap products. Putting aside the wretch factor, could this really be done?

Lye is an alkali that, when mixed with fatty acids, produces soap. The human body contains sodium, oxygen and hydrogen, the elements that form lye; one dead human body could produce about six ounces of lye when properly mixed.

Additionally, a 150-pound person with 20% body fat could provide 30 pounds of fat. Modern soap products include oils and scents that make the soap creamier and smell better, but these ingredients are not technically needed to produce soap.

If our recipe uses a mixture of 15% lye/85% fat, the lye and fat in one dead human body could produce about two and a half pounds of soap. Assuming some fat loss after unwanted fat byproducts are skimmed during the preparation, each of our bodies could produce 7-10 bars of soap.

Cutting Through the Fat

A bar of soap allegedly crafted using fat liposuctioned from Italian prime minister Silvio Berlusconi sold for 15,000 euros ($18,000 US) at an art auction in 2005. Artist Gianni Monti's work, entitled "Clean Hands," was reportedly bought by a private Swiss collector. No word on whether the Swiss collector actually used the pricey soap, or if the prime minister cleaned up from the sale.

Soap Facts

The ingredients for Babylonian soap (water, alkali, and cassia oil) were found on a 4,000-year old clay tablet.

Ancient Egyptians bathed in a mixture of alkaline salt, animal fat and vegetable oils.

American settlers poured hot water over wood ashes to produce alkali potash that was boiled with animal fats to make an effective, though harsh and foul smelling soap.

Body Odor is the Pits

Use #13: Antiperspirant Deodorant

Sweat doesn't smell. A common misperception, but sweat doesn't have a scent. Perspiration is the body's way to cool us when the temperature (or our tension level) is high, and sweat interacts with the living bacteria that is always present on our bodies. When the bacteria dies it mixes with perspiration to create body odor.

Antiperspirants limit the body from emitting moisture by blocking the sweat glands with a gel plug. Early antiperspirants used zinc to dry the armpits, while later formulas employed aluminum chloride and many variations of aluminum zirconium. Deodorants and antiperspirants can be rolled or sprayed on, and come in lots of varieties for our sweaty, smelly pleasure.

Don't Sweat the Details

Aluminum and chlorine are two ingredients found in the human body that are also used in antiperspirants. The human body contains 95 grams of chlorine, but just 60 milligrams of aluminum. One dead human body could produce 125 mg. of aluminum chloride, a compound that composes anywhere from 10%-25% of the active ingredients in a container of antiperspirant.

A 2.6 oz. (73 gram) container of antiperspirant stick contains at least 7.3 grams of aluminum chloride, requiring the combined chlorine and aluminum contents of about 58 dead human bodies to provide the active ingredients in one stick of antiperspirant deodorant. You may think that's an excessive number, but it's really nothing to raise a stink about.

One Smelly Emperor

Antiperspirant deodorants wouldn't have gone over well with Napoleon Bonaparte, who was said to rarely bathe and masked his stench with copious amounts of cologne. Worse off was his wife, Josephine, who he urged to abstain from bathing so he could bask in her natural fragrance. No wonder he was banished to his own island.

Deodorant Facts

Ancient Egyptians bathed in scented water and rubbed citric and cinnamon-tinged ointments under their arms. They also shaved their armpits, which reduces the breeding area for underarm bacteria.

Body odor smells different depending on the person emitting it. Age, gender, diet and general health affect the odor's pungency, which is why some people smell dandy after a 10K run while others reek after changing the bottle on a water cooler.

The Whole Tooth, and Nothing But the Tooth
Use #14: Toothpaste

Sodium fluoride, which strengthens teeth and helps prevent tooth decay, is a common ingredient in toothpaste; the sodium and fluorine in one dead human body could make 5.75 grams of sodium fluoride. Toothpaste contains only a small amount of sodium fluoride, about .243% of the total ingredients.

One 232 gram (8.2 oz) tube of toothpaste contains just .56 grams of sodium fluoride. One dead human body could provide the sodium fluoride content for ten tubes of toothpaste…unless you swallow your toothpaste, in which case you may contain a little bit more.

Toothpaste Facts

Vinegar, volcanic stone, baking soda and human urine all have been used to clean teeth.

Early Egyptians and Romans cleaned their teeth with "chewing sticks," special twigs similar to tooth picks that are still used in certain parts of the world today.

China invented the earliest known toothbrush 500 years ago. The modern toothbrush was inspired by China's invention, popularized in Europe during the late 1700's.

Drink to Your Dental Health
Use #15: Sodium Fluoride Water

Scientists in the 1930's discovered that people who drank water containing naturally occurring fluoride had fewer cavities. Man-made fluoridation was first tested in Newburgh, New York and Grand Rapids, Michigan in 1945; by the 1950's public health officials recommended its widespread use. Today, half of the US population now consumes fluoridated water.

Fluoridation involves some risk, which has discouraged many communities from adopting the practice. Excessive fluoride consumption can lead to bone and teeth damage, while some scientists speculate that fluoridation may exacerbate kidney disease. Though these risks are rare, communities often reject fluoridation in spite of the considerable benefits.

The EPA allows a maximum amount of four parts per million of sodium fluoride in drinking water, with a recommended level of two parts per million (or two milligrams of sodium fluoride per liter of water). If we assume a sodium fluoride level of two parts per million, one dead human body could provide the sodium fluoride content for 759 gallons of water.

Filling a Void
Use #16: Dental Fillings

If toothpaste and sodium fluoride-spiked water don't prevent your teeth from falling out, you may need a filling. A dental filling seals the portion of a tooth that has deteriorated due to tooth decay. Fillings can be made out of a variety of materials, including dental amalgam (mercury, silver, tin, copper and other metals), glass and quartz composites, or a gold alloy.

A gold alloy filling is made out of gold and one or more other metals, like copper. Small amounts of gold and copper are found in the human body, with copper (72 mg) more common than gold (0.2 mg). The composition of the alloy can vary, so we'll assume 75% gold/25% copper.

Assuming an average filling size of one gram, the combined gold and copper contents of about 3,750 dead human bodies would be needed to make one filling. You could make a real killing with a filling, provided you can dig up that many donors.

The Silver Lining

The human body also contains the materials to make a dental amalgam. Assuming a typical composition of mercury, silver, copper, and tin, we'd need the contributions of about 175 dead human bodies to make one dental amalgam.

Chapter Four
Surgical Procedures

Peter Lorre played a brilliant surgeon obsessed with an opera singer in the film *Mad Love* (1935). When the singer's pianist husband damages his hands in a freak accident, she pleads with Lorre to help. He responds by supplying her husband with the hands of an executed murderer who killed his victims with knives. Soon enough, the husband develops his own unhealthy fixation for knives and worries that he may become a murderer, too.

Homicidal tendencies are not a typical result of hand transplants, but Lorre & Co. deserve credit for being ahead of the curve. The first successful, short-term hand transplant took place in 1998, though the hand was removed three years later after the patient complained that it felt like a dead man's hand--which it was, from a donor who died in a motorcycle accident. Dead human bodies also contain materials used to perform surgeries and replace joints, as the following examples demonstrate.

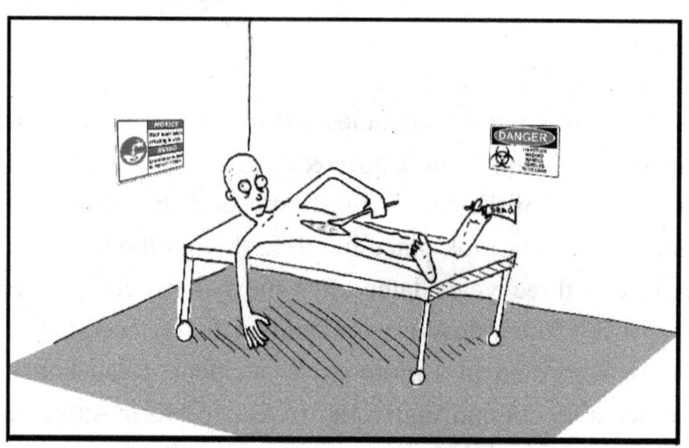
NOTICE
DANGER
DEAD

Da Vinci's Dissections

Use #17: Dissecting Dead Human Bodies

A painter, sculptor, inventor, architect, human anatomist, and all-around handy guy, Leonardo Da Vinci was the ultimate Renaissance man. His exploration of the human body was revolutionary, and controversial.

Da Vinci performed dissections of human bodies for almost 20 years and kept meticulous, detailed sketches of his observations. Human body dissections were considered blasphemous at the time, but Leonardo's reputation and reluctance to publish his journals allowed him to work largely unnoticed. He dissected dozens of cadavers during this period, mostly criminals and victims of old age.

Working by candlelight in the dead of night, Da Vinci determined the relationship between muscles, tendons, joints and bones, later describing bodily functions in mechanical terms. He employed a layered technique in his drawings depicting human musculature, isolated individual body parts to create more precise drawings, and correctly theorized how most of the body's internal organs worked.

Cholesterol Crusader

While dissecting the corpse of an old man believed to be about 100 years old, Da Vinci noticed the man's hardened heart vessels and decided the cause to be an excessive diet, in comparison to the body of a young child he also dissected. By deducing that the old man's death was brought on by the food he ate, Da Vinci identified a common health hazard widely known today but unheard of during his time. Always the trailblazer, Da Vinci himself was a vegetarian.

Da Vinci's anatomical drawings were lost for hundreds of years after his death, allowing others to perform similar experiments and receive credit for reaching the same conclusions. But the primitive surroundings in which he worked, scandalous subject matter, and exactness of his drawings are a testament to his unique spirit.

Da Vinci's work was cut short when strict religious conventions finally prompted Pope Leo X to ban his human dissections. His work, both literally and figuratively, cut too deep for the times he lived.

The Final Cut
Use #18: Tantalum-Coated Scalpels

Tantalum is a rare metal that is resistant to corrosion and doesn't react with bodily fluids, making it ideal for surgical equipment. The human body, a remarkable resource of unexpected elements, contains .2 milligrams of tantalum.

Danfoss Tantalum Technologies sells tantalum coating for use in medical and industrial parts, with tantalum coating thickness measured in microns.

Minuscule amounts of other metals may be included in the coating, but we'll assume a 100% pure tantalum composition for our purpose.

If we coat an entire 13 cm. scalpel with a modest tantalum thickness of 10 microns, we would need approximately 32 milligrams of tantalum, or the contributions of about 160 dead human bodies. If we merely coat the blade, we would need approximately five milligrams of tantalum from 25 dead human bodies.

Bionic Body
Use #19: Titanium Joint Replacements

In "The Six Million Dollar Man," Lee Majors played a test pilot who nearly dies in a plane crash. "We can rebuild him. We have the technology," the voice-over intoned, so the US government equipped him with cybernetic technology and springy sound effects, allowing him to battle foreign agents, diabolical conspirators and, in one memorable episode, Sasquatch.

You may never have the chance to battle mythic forest creatures or jump from a building to the sound of jazzy theme music, but the technology to rebuild you does exist. All you need is the proper replacement parts.

jointreplacement.com offers information for those needing shoulder, finger, hip, knee and ankle replacement surgery. Many materials are used to construct replacement joints, including cement, plastic, and a variety of metal alloys that may include titanium.

Titanium is ideal for joint replacements due to its strength, high-corrosion resistance and biocompatibility. If you've ever felt a little bionic yourself (or if you've ever heard sound effects while jumping out of the shower), you can credit the 20 mg of titanium found in the human body.

By the way, with an October 2005 value of $23.00 per pound, the titanium alloy content of approximately 5,916,422,099 dead human bodies could produce six million dollars worth of titanium. That's nearly the entire world's population. Whatever ABC was paying Lee Majors, he was worth it.

Chapter Five
Intensive Care

"I'm dying with the aid of too many physicians."

attributed to Alexander the Great

Alexander's sentiments notwithstanding, serious medical conditions require treatment from a medical professional, and many of the materials used to treat severe illnesses can be found in the human body.

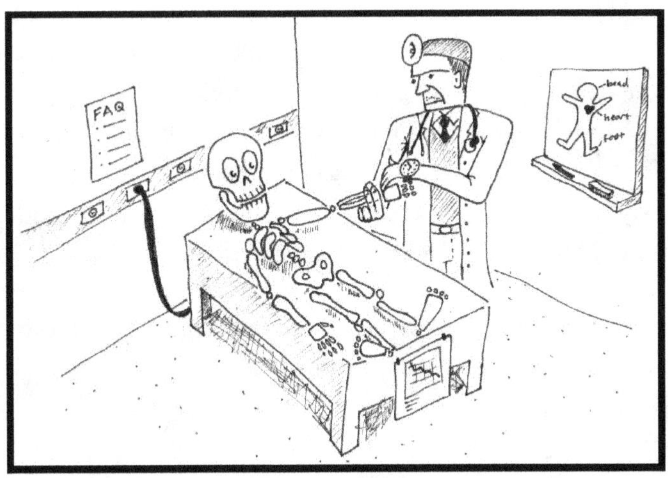

What Doesn't Kill You Makes You Stronger
Use #20: Trisenox Leukemia Treatment

Chocolate and alcohol are guilty pleasures that, when taken in the proper amounts, are said to have nutritional value. While it's likely the marketing gurus at Hershey's and Jim Beam have done a lot to spread this information, it is true that small amounts of otherwise unhealthy things can sometimes be good for us.

You'd be hard-pressed to find arsenic sold in a candy wrapper or liquor bottle, but arsenic trioxide, an arsenic-oxygen compound manufactured under the brand name Trisenox, is used to treat leukemia. It's not known exactly how Trisenox works, but it's believed that arsenic trioxide causes cancer cells to undergo apoptosis (self-destruction). Arsenic is a toxic substance, so there's a significant danger with this treatment.

Per the FDA, Trisenox is administered intravenously in a 10 mL solution containing 10 mg of arsenic trioxide. The human body contains both oxygen (43 kg) and arsenic (15 mg). Put together, the human body could produce roughly 18 mg of arsenic trioxide, more than enough for one Trisenox treatment.

Have you ever met someone who was bearable only in small doses? Blame arsenic.

Nature's Balance
Use #21: Bipolar Treatment

Over two million people in the United States suffer from manic depression, while millions more are estimated to be affected but undiagnosed. Also known as bipolar disorder, the illness is distinguished by extreme mood swings, causing the patient to oscillate between manic emotional "highs" and depressive "lows."

The frequently prescribed chemical compound lithium carbonate is available under a variety of brand names. The ingredients for lithium carbonate--lithium, oxygen and carbon--are also found in the human body. One dead human body could produce 35 mg of lithium carbonate.

Nine dead human bodies could provide the lithium, oxygen and carbon to manufacture one 300 mg dose of lithium carbonate. The prescribed daily amount will vary from patient to patient, but if we assume a daily total of 900 mg, the lithium carbonate content of about 26 dead human bodies could fill a one-day prescription.

Bipolar Facts

It's not known what causes manic depression, though occurrences between family members suggest a genetic link.

Pain Relief

Use #22: Quadramet Cancer Treatment

Cancer is an indiscriminate disease. It attacks men and women equally, young and old, all over the world. Cancer is caused by out of control cell growth, which damages and destroys healthy tissue. It can attack any part of the body, and then spread (metastasize) to other areas of the body.

When cancer metastasizes and infects a patient's bones, a doctor may prescribe Quadramet to relieve the pain. Quadramet is a radiopharmaceutical containing a radioactive form of the element samarium that can alleviate bone pain after just one injection. Pain relief usually begins within a few weeks after treatment and lasts for 12 to 16 weeks.

The human body contains samarium, too, though not in radioactive form. The amount of samarium in a dosage of Quadramet will vary depending on the patient's body size, but if the 50 micrograms of samarium in one human body could be used in Quadramet, it would be enough to supply the 5-46 micrograms needed for one treatment.

This Film is X-Rayed
Use #23: Beryllium Foil

An X-ray, just like visible light, is a form of electromagnetic energy. The way we see the world depends on how light interacts with the objects around us. For example, visible light waves pass through glass, but are absorbed by opaque material like wood. X-rays do the same thing but are not absorbed by as many materials.

This allows X-rays to be used in medical examinations. Much of the human body is made of soft tissue, which does not absorb X-ray energy, but human bone does absorb X-rays, making the human skeleton visible (or illuminated) when photographed during an X-ray machine exam.

In order for X-ray machines to function properly, visible light must be filtered out so that only X-ray waves are detected by the camera. This can be achieved by using beryllium foil. 36 micrograms of beryllium can be found in the human body.

Girmet Ltd. produces beryllium foil with a beryllium content of 99.8%, in addition to small amounts of these elements: Oxygen; Carbon; Aluminum; Manganese; Iron; Lead; Chromium; Magnesium; Nickel; Boron; Silicon; Molybdenum; Antimony; Tin; Calcium; Vanadium; Thallium; Copper; Zinc; Cadmium; Tungsten; Tantalum; Arsenic; Sodium; Niobium; Phosphorus; Lanthanum; Gadolinium; Cobalt; Cerium.

One dead human body contains all of these ingredients, though the stingy amount of beryllium dwarfs the contributions of the others. Girmet Ltd. sells beryllium foil by the square inch, but if measured by weight one dead human body could produce approximately 36 micrograms of beryllium foil.

Chapter Six
After Death

"I intend to live forever, or die trying."

attributed to Groucho Marx

Sadly, Groucho died trying, but that doesn't mean you have to. There are a variety of ways a dead human body can live on, whether as a science tool, through organ donation, or frozen for future resuscitation.

Them Bones
Use #24: Classroom Skeletons

Is there a harsher reminder of human mortality than a skeleton, held together by wire, hanging in a classroom? These cryptic creations are usually constructed of plastic, but for the lucky student whose health professor has enough funding, your classroom skeleton might be the real thing.

If you would like to purchase a daily reminder of your impending death, visit anatomy-resources.com and search for "real human bones" on the skeletal system page. But be warned…a genuine human skeleton will cost you an arm and a leg.

For $4995.00, you can purchase a complete, hand assembled human skeleton with removable arms and museum-quality features. It comes equipped with a spring loaded jaw for exhibiting dental detail, a hook for hanging, a skeleton bone identification chart, and a zippered dust cover. Costumes and props sold separately.

If that price is too steep, you could purchase a human skull instead. A first class human skull with teeth intact will run you $1595.00. A second class human skull (with minor flaws, some discoloration and less teeth) costs $949.95, while a third class skull (not as exact, due to numerous flaws, but darn atmospheric) can be had for the bargain-basement price of $759.95. For an extra $90 bucks you can add false teeth, and maybe a wig to spruce it up.

Due to demand and limited availability, expect a three year wait for your skeleton. While death waits for no man, man will find that death has a waiting list.

Can You Spare a Kidney?
Use #25: Organ Donation

Human body and organ donation has a long history, including many alleged attempts dating back thousands of years. The first successful bone grafts were first documented in 1668 and 1682, while the first modern skin autograft (transplanting one's own skin to another part of the body) took place in 1822.

1881 was a red-letter date in organ donation history, when a surgeon used skin from a cadaver as a temporary graft for a burn victim who was leaning against a metal door when it was struck by lightning. The skin graft allowed the victim's own skin to heal underneath.

The first successful kidney transplant from a living donor took place in 1954, followed eight years later by the first successful kidney transplant from a deceased donor. New ways of determining tissue types and drugs that suppress the immune system made these advancements possible, and led the way to the first successful liver transplant in 1967. The first successful heart transplant took place that same year, taken from the body of an 18-year old who died in a car accident.

How to Become an Organ Donor

According to the Mayo Clinic, more than 95,000 people are on the U.S. organ transplant waiting list, desperately in need of hearts, lungs, kidneys, livers, pancreases, intestines or bone marrow. Nearly 6,000 people died in 2006 waiting for an organ transplant, or one every 90 minutes.

Signing a donor card or indicating on your driver's license that you wish to be an organ donor are not always legally binding. Informing your next of kin that you wish to be an organ donor, signing a state or national donor registry, or assigning power of attorney to someone you trust are the best ways to insure that your wishes will be carried out.

How to Become a Science Project

The necessary steps for donating your entire body to science are a bit trickier, since laws on how bodies may be donated and utilized after death vary from state to state. In *Anatomical Gift: Whole Body Donation Guide*, author Regina Lee offers worksheets, forms, certificates and other documents that should be filled out by those who wish to donate their bodies for medical research or organ donation. As Lee explains, even though a deceased person may bequeath his body may not stop family members from stopping the donation.

Lee also lists over 100 medical programs around the country that accept cadaver contributions and details how the cadavers will be used, though these institutions often have standards for what types of corpses they will accept. Bodies of people who died under the age of 18, obese or emaciated bodies, those that died as a result of suicide or a communicable disease, or otherwise tampered with or decomposing bodies are often not accepted, so if you want your mortal vessel to sail on after you die, you had better maintain the upkeep.

Organ Donation Facts

In the ancient text Samhita (written 2100-2700 years ago), Indian author Sushrota described facial reconstructions using skin grafts.

The Chinese doctor Pien Ch-iao claimed over 2500 years ago that he exchanged the heart of a strong but weak-willed man with the heart of a weak but strong willed man in order to achieve balance.

Roman Catholic mythology describes two saints in the 3rd or 4th century who replaced a soldier's gangrene leg with that of a fallen enemy.

Giving Death the Cold Shoulder
Use #26: Cryonics

If you haven't come to grips with your impending mortality (or if you hope the future holds more promise than the present), medical science has found a way to delay the inevitable: cryonics.

Cryonics supporters believe dead people might

someday be revived and cured of whatever killed them. Modern medicine cannot heal all diseases, but the future holds infinite promise…at least, that's the promise the cryonically preserved are counting on.

Included in that promise is the expectation that the cryonics process can be reversed and the damage from the process can be repaired, but those details are left to future scientists and doctors to figure out. Modern cryonics has its hands full with the actual practice of preserving dead human bodies…like yours.

Frozen Fish Sticks and You on Aisle 10

Shortly after you die a cryonics specialist will arrive to prepare your body for the big chill. While CPR is administered on your dead body in order to maintain circulation, you are injected with a solution that reduces blood clotting and minimizes the formation of ice crystals that could damage your system (technically speaking, cryonic preservation keeps a body very cold, not frozen). You will then be taken to a cryonics facility, which for legal reasons may be classified as a cemetery, albeit a temporary one.

You have the option of either a full body preservation or only having your head preserved, assuming that future medical science will be able to grow you a new body. In either case, your head is in for a rude awakening when the extreme cold causes the phenomena known as an acoustic fracturing event. More on that in a moment…

Your bodily remains (or head without a body)

are cooled to the temperature of liquid nitrogen (about -200 degrees C), then placed in a sack similar to a sleeping bag and inserted into a stainless steel tank resembling a giant thermos. The center portion of the container is filled with liquid nitrogen, with safety precautions in place to keep the cool air flowing in case of a power outage. Your body will be stored upside down so that your noggin will be the last thing to spoil in case of a premature thaw.

Which is considerate, in light of the trauma your head has already experienced. As your body temperature drops below freezing, your brain will harden and crack, maybe multiple times, making a popping sound referred to earlier as an acoustic fracturing event. Scientists are working to reduce this phenomena, though you shouldn't be too concerned if your brain fractures into several pieces. Remember, future medicine can cure anything, even a broken cerebellum.

Cryonic preservation will run you between $35,000 and $60,000 for just your head, or as much as $150,000 for your entire body. If you're not particularly enamored with your head or your body, you can opt to preserve a sample of your DNA instead (perhaps with the expectation that future medical science can cure ugliness, too).

Does This Qualify as a Use?

Sure, since you plan on using your once-dead human body after you're reanimated. But if the thought of waking up a thousand years from now after medical science has discovered a cure for that strange rash that killed you isn't impressive enough, also remember that your body contains nitrogen. Your dead body could provide some of the liquid nitrogen needed to chill your dead body. Cool, huh?

Cryonics in Popular Media

Since the publication of Robert Ettinger's book *The Prospect of Immortality* in the early 1960's, cryonics has been celebrated, exploited but mostly lampooned in books, films and television shows.

Michael A. Black's mystery novel *Freeze Me, Tender* involves the shenanigans of a supposedly cryogenically frozen rock star, while the plot of David Masurek's science fiction novel *Counting Heads* includes, yup, cryogenically frozen heads. Woody Allen had a lot of fun with cryonics in his 1972 comedy film *Sleepers* by exploring the culture shock of a modern day man who wakes up in the future, while Matt Groening's futuristic television comedy *Futurama* often featured animated cameos by historical figures whose heads live on in glass jars.

If the prospect of living in a glass jar doesn't sound very appealing, remember...there's always mummification.

Cryonics Facts

If the thought of living in the future without your favorite pet sounds unbearable, some cryonics facilities also offer to preserve animals.

Robert Ettinger, a pioneer in cryonics philosophy, is the guiding light behind the Cryonics Institute (cryonics.org), one of a few organizations that offer cryonic services. If you can't afford the preservation fee, the Cryonics Institute and other organizations suggest taking out a life insurance policy and bequeathing the amount to them. Package deals are available for families at a discounted rate, because there's nothing better than a bargain...even in the afterlife.

Chapter Seven
Cannibalism

In the summer of 1846, a group of pioneers struck out from Illinois to California, hoping to make new lives for themselves in a new land. But they were given bad directions and got bogged down in Utah, where infighting delayed their progress by weeks. Winter approached, and heavy snow blocked their passage by the time they reached the Sierra Nevada mountains. 17 members continued to California to bring help; only ten succeeded. Many of those left behind fell victim to the harsh cold and starvation. Some of the survivors turned to cannibalism.

So it went for the Donner Party, named after its chief organizer, George Donner. Only 40 of the original 87 pioneers survived. It's hard to say how many of the survivors consumed human flesh, or how many were consumed. Records are sketchy, and the survivors probably weren't forthcoming with the details.

But we won't let that deter us. While most of us will never taste human flesh, simple curiosity begs the question: what do we taste like? The editors of *Bon Appétit* have never tackled that one.

In addition, the human body is chockfull of nutrients and contains the raw materials to make many common food items. Do you still find cannibalism disturbing? Don't let it eat away at you.

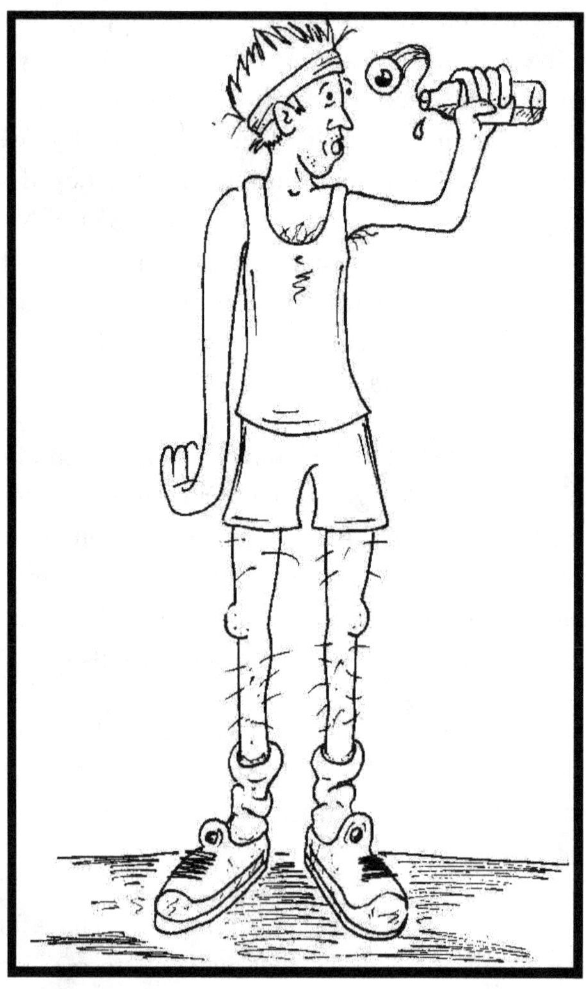

You Are Who You Eat
Use #27: Eating the Dead

Ambition leads me not only farther than any other man has been before me, but as far as I think it possible for man to go.

Captain James Cook (1728-1779)

British Naval Explorer

Cook commanded three major voyages in his lifetime, during which he discovered corners of the world no one had ever seen. He crisscrossed the Pacific Ocean, charted new island systems and created groundbreaking maps of Australia and other countries. On his second voyage he sailed south for three years in search of a mythic southern polar region until he finally discovered icebergs, suggesting the existence of the South Pole. Though he failed to accomplish the goals of his third voyage, he did conduct a thorough expedition of America's northwest coast and the arctic ocean.

Cook was known for his scientific approach to cartography. He also treated his crew well, and had a gentle touch with the natives he met during his travels. He made several stops in New Guinea, Tonga and the Tahiti islands, chronicling the local customs--including cannibalism. His deft handling of foreign people contributed to his reputation as one of the greatest explorers of all time...but a man's reputation will carry him for only so long.

Cook bit off more than he could chew on his third and final voyage, when he discovered and named the Hawaiian Islands but failed to find an arctic passageway between the Atlantic and Pacific oceans. He returned to Hawaii in late 1778, where he became embroiled in a dispute between his men and the indigenous Hawaiian people over a boat stolen from his vessel, the *Discovery*.

The dispute didn't end well for Cook, whose mutilated, dismembered body was recovered by his crew mates and buried at sea. The sorry state of his remains suggested that he may have been cannibalized, an ironic end for someone who was dedicated to exploring new worlds: he was devoured by the very people who consumed his life.

Ever been tempted to nosh on your own body? If so, you may suffer from autosarcophagy, the practice of eating oneself, a rare phenomena manifested in fingernail eating, compulsive hair chewing, and ingesting one's own blood or skin.

Or maybe you're just curious. There are many historical anecdotes that describe the taste of human flesh, most of them fantastical and many contradictory. A modern anecdote comes from William Seabrook, a New York Times reporter in the 1930's who spent time with the indigenous Gueré people of Western Africa, hoping to provide a firsthand account of what human meat tastes like.

“The raw meat, in appearance, was firm, slightly course-textured rather than smooth,” Seabrook described when offered the chance to taste human meat. “In raw texture, both to the eye and to the touch, it resembled good beef.” He described the fatty content as clearly resembling beef, as opposed to pork, then described the raw aroma "characteristic...of any good fresh meat of the larger domestic animals.”

He prepared a seasoned stew, rice, and a bottle of wine, but wished to taste the meat first using simple preparation and minimal seasoning. "When the roast began to brown and the steak to turn blackish on the outside, I cut into them to have a look at the partially cooked interior. It had turned quite paler than beef would turn. It was turning grayish as veal or lamb would…it was nearly done and it looked and smelled good to eat.”

He took a bite, realizing he had bluffed himself into trying human meat, then said, “At any rate, it was perfectly good to eat! At any rate, it had no weird, startling, or unholy special flavor.” After another bite he spoke with certainty about the taste. “It was a mild, good meat with no other sharply defined or highly characteristic taste such as for instance goat, high game, and pork have…veal is the one meat to which this meat is accurately comparable.”

Seabrook’s firsthand account of cannibal culture thrilled the reading public’s hunger for far-flung native life, and was repeated in magazine and newspaper stories. But the tribal members who hosted Seabrook during a ritualistic African dinner fed him ape meat instead of human meat, which defeated Seabrook’s goal of sampling human flesh in a native environment.

So Seabrook traveled to France where he had friends in the local medical community who provided him with cadaver meat for his experiment, which informed the description in his book. "I feel that it would be unfair, unsporting, and ungrateful to involve and identify too closely the individual friends who made my experiment possible." No doubt his friends in the French medical community appreciated his gentlemanly discretion.

If Seabrook hasn't tempted you to taste human flesh, consider this simple assertion from Karl Würf's cheeky cookbook, *To Serve Man: A Cookbook for People*: "Why eat Man?" Würf asks in the introduction. "The harder question is, why not? After all, Man is a large, plentiful (some say *too* plentiful) animal…And, above all, man is *available*." Würf says that a choice human specimen (weighing a lean 240 pounds) could yield 60% edible meat.

To Serve Man offers a variety of recipes to please any palette. *Person Kebab*, for example, requires three pounds of man, cooked on a spit-roast with mushrooms, sweet bell peppers and pineapple squares. Or how about this recipe for *Sautéed Brains*: start with a precooked human brain, fry in a skillet with ¼ pound human body fat and ½ pound lean human meat slices. When the mixture is crisp, sauté the brains in hot oil until brown.

Despite the cookbook's title, it's easy to imagine using ordinary animal meat in any of the recipes (except for the sautéed brains, which is exotic any way you slice it). Instead, consider this authentic recipe for Gueré Stew, told to William Seabrook: Cut the human meat into fist-sized portions and boil in a modest amount of water; when the stew simmers down, add quantities of rice.

The Gueré people strongly discourage using bananas or any other form of vegetable, as these common ingredients don't go well with Gueré Stew. Who knew cannibals were so finicky?

Good, and Good for You
Use #28: Human Body Nutrients

Cannibal or not, you still need proper nutrients in your diet. One dead human body can help you achieve that goal.

Potassium is an important nutrient that, among other functions, can help lower your risk of hypertension. One dead human body contains 140 grams of potassium. That's equivalent to the potassium content of 310 bananas.

Calcium, which is critical in the formation of bones and teeth, is necessary for all living organisms. One dead human body contains one kilogram of calcium, equal to the calcium content of 3,509 servings of milk.

Human beings need about 2.4 grams of sodium a day, far less than most people consume. One dead human body contains 100 grams of sodium, comparable to 14 tablespoons of salt.

I Could Use a Little Flavor
Use #29: Salt

Sodium and chlorine form sodium chloride, also known as table salt. If combined, the sodium and chlorine in one dead human body could produce 157 grams of table salt.

According to the consumer group Consensus Action on Salt and Health (CASH), that's enough salt to flavor 56 Big Mac/Fries/Soft Drink meals from McDonalds. If you prefer Chicken McNuggets with your fries and drink, one dead human body could provide the salt content for 105 meals.

Most people eat too much salt, so please keep the human salt-flavored Big Macs to a minimum.

Good to the Last Drop
Use #30: Water

Water is the most abundant resource in the human body, so it stands to reason that reusing the water in a dead body is the best way to contribute to the recycling movement. Refreshing, too.

If the hydrogen and oxygen in one dead human body were combined, it could produce 12 gallons of water.

In the world of long-distance running, the Badwater Ultramarathon is considered the world's toughest foot race. Competitors run non-stop for 30+ hours in blistering, 130-degree heat through Death Valley, California. Proper hydration is a must.

An average runner requires about a quart of water every hour. The water content of one dead human body could keep the runners in the Badwater Ultramarathon hydrated for over 40 hours, more than enough to win the race. Death Valley has claimed many lives, but here's an instance where death can get the better of the valley.

Chapter Eight
Death by the Dead

A Mongolian folk story tells the bizarre tale of the “biting corpse,” in which a wife sneaks food past her new husband in order to feed her deceased husband, whose body rests behind a burial rock. Upon feeding him a spoonful, the corpse bites off the spoon; with his next bite he chomps off the wife’s nose.

That’s ungrateful behavior, but dead bodies have never been known for their civility. Superstitions in which the dead feed upon the living and rob them of their life force have long played a part in vampire and zombie legends, but dead bodies needn’t be animated to prove fatal, as the following examples show.

The French Underground
Use #31: The Catacombs of Paris

The city of Paris conceals a secret in its underbelly: hundreds of miles of tunnels burrowed underneath the city. The first tunnels were excavated 2000 years ago by Ancient Romans searching for gypsum and limestone for use in building construction. Future generations hollowed out more passageways to create famous landmarks like the cathedral of Notre Dame and the Louvre. Excavations were halted in the 18th century when cave-ins caused entire buildings to crumble, prompting city officials to fortify or close the tunnels.

The empty tunnels, or catacombs, proved useful in the late 1700's when neighborhood cemeteries grew overcrowded. Generations of family plots housed in small church graveyards caused some cemeteries to rise as high as ten feet above street level. Human waste from the exposed graves began to infect the nearby population, in some cases causing death. To solve the overcrowding, millions of human remains were removed from the old cemeteries and transferred to the many caverns tucked deep within the labyrinth-like catacomb system.

Death Brings Death

How does a dead human body cause death? When a human body begins decomposing, the same elements that once kept that body alive are released as toxic compounds that devour the corpse and pose a threat to the living.

The human body's digestive system contains bacteria that break down nutrients during a person's lifetime. The body's immune system no longer balances the corrosive effects of this bacteria after we die, leading to bacterial consumption of the internal organs.

The bacteria multiply within a few days and begin devouring tissue and cells, causing body fluids to flood the internal cavities. Ammonia, a caustic and hazardous compound, accumulates in the lungs shortly after death, later exiting through the nose and mouth.

Other noxious, foul-smelling gases like hydrogen sulphide, methane, cadaverine, putrescine and carbon dioxide are also released--dangerous for humans to inhale but attractive to the many insects who begin laying eggs on the dead body. Insect larvae promptly appear, causing further disintegration while releasing even more toxic gases into the nearby atmosphere.

After a couple of weeks, bacteria is competing with insects in an all-you-can-eat smorgasbord, producing more gases, fluids, and reasons to consider a cremation burial. The corpse is now a pestilence machine, harboring dangerous gases, disease-carrying bugs and soil-permeating body juices that can harm the living and make the surrounding area difficult to inhabit.

In a month's time the dead body ferments and produces mold, while butyric acid (normally found in rancid butter, parmesan cheese and vomit) exudes from the corpse. Putrefaction slowly winds down as bacterial activity decreases and any remaining gases and liquids extinguish from the body until all that remains is a dry collection of bones…waiting to be arranged in a lively pattern like those found in the Parisian catacombs.

Catacomb Facts

The catacomb creators built elaborate displays using the remains taken from old cemeteries. Skulls and femurs arranged in ghoulish patterns line huge subterranean rooms, some containing graffiti dating back to the French Revolution and World War II.

Aside from the skeletons, the catacomb system has also hosted bizarre social gatherings. Charles X threw wild parties in the catacombs, while more recent soirees include a group that secretly sets up movie screenings and seminars in the larger corridors.

The catacombs were made off limits in 1955, though it's difficult for law enforcement to police the many cavernous, winding tunnels. Some of the chambers are hidden so deep that explorers risk losing their lives to catch a glimpse of those who have already passed.

An estimated six million skeletons are believed to occupy the catacomb system, though only a handful can be seen in the officially sanctioned public passageways.

Contagious Corpses

Use #32: The Ebola Virus

Here's a nasty way to cash in your chips: the Ebola virus begins with a high fever, headache, muscle and joint pain, plus a stomach ache accompanied by weakness, exhaustion, and dizziness--symptoms often associated with the flu. Then diarrhea and vomiting blood set in, while hypotension (low blood pressure) foreshadows organ damage and internal hemorrhaging. External bleeding of the orifices begins within a week, and old wounds and injection sites refuse to heal, finally resulting in death from organ failure or hypovolemic shock (lack of blood) for up to 90% of those infected.

If that's not your idea of a fun vacation, you may want to avoid the Democratic Republic of the Congo, Sudan, and a number of other African countries where the Ebola virus and its many strains were first discovered. Ebola ravaged the gorilla population in Central Africa, then killed hundreds of humans starting in the 1970's. The mysterious disease is believed to be sustained between viral outbreaks by fruit bat colonies.

A corpse infected with the Ebola virus remains contagious for as long as the virus is present in bodily fluids. Local burial rituals don't always neutralize the threat of infection, requiring medical personnel to implement special disposal procedures. About 30% of those who treated Ebola victims during a previous outbreak in Sudan also fell victim to the virus, so you can imagine the vested interest health care workers have in dependable dead body disposal.

Silver Surfing
Use #33: Mercury Poisoning

Science class film strips once showed early 20th century scientists playfully floating atop huge vats of liquid mercury. The threat of mercury poisoning was considered so minor that mercury was once used in textiles to preserve fabrics. Little did people know the physiological and psychological effects mercury exposure had on textile workers, leading to the infamous "mad hatter" phenomena.

It's now known that even modest mercury exposure can be hazardous and potentially fatal. According to the Environmental Protection Agency, mercury poisoning can impair peripheral vision, cause disturbing sensations in the hands, feet, and mouth, and impede coordination of movement. It can also impair speech, hearing and walking, weaken muscles, cause skin rashes, and prompt mood swings, memory loss and mental disturbance. Hardly worth swimming laps in a vat of mercury, is it?

The threat is so severe that pregnant women are warned not to eat more than one serving of freshwater fish a week due to mercury pollution, while the mercury content from one broken thermometer can contaminate an entire room. A dead human body contains six milligrams of mercury--a paltry amount, though victims of mercury poisoning sometimes ingest small amounts over a period of time before finally succumbing to the poison.

Mercury Facts

Famous individuals who may have been poisoned by mercury include:

Qin Shi Huang Di, the first Emperor of Unified China, who took mercury pills in an effort to achieve eternal life;

Niccoló Paganini, the famous violin virtuoso;

Louisa May Alcott, author of Little Women, *who received mercury-laden calomel treatment for typhoid fever that she contracted while serving as a Civil War nurse;*

Samuel Richardson, 18th century writer;

Harry Houdini--scores of books have been written about his mysterious death and possible return from the afterlife. If he returns, maybe he'll reveal how he died.

You're a Bitter Pill
Use #34: Poisons Found in the Human Body

Lead Poisoning

Lead serves no biological purpose in the human body, but about 120 mg can be found in the skeletal system. A poison's potency depends on how it enters the body: lead that is ingested with food often passes out of the digestive system without causing any harm, but lead injected into the bloodstream can be fatal in small amounts.

Lead poisoning was identified thousands of years ago by the ancient Greek poet and physician Nicander, who described symptoms including hallucinations and paralysis. Accidental lead poisoning was common long before Nicander's time because of lead's popularity as a malleable, easy to melt metal.

Lead Fact

Nicander erroneously suggested using a laxative to cure lead poisoning.

Arsenic

Ancient Roman politicians, notorious for poisoning their rivals, pioneered the use of arsenic as an agent of death, a fate that doomed Napoleon Bonaparte centuries later. After Napoleon was banished to St. Helena island in 1815, he slowly became ill with stomach cancer and died six years later. It's speculated that the wallpaper in his study, colored with a green dye containing arsenic, gradually poisoned him to death.

Arsenic's notoriety later inspired a famous Broadway comedy, *Arsenic and Old Lace,* about two old spinsters who take in boarders, then murder them to collect their pensions. As little as 200 mg of arsenic can be lethal, much more than the 15 mg of arsenic found in one person, requiring the contributions of about 13 dead human bodies for one lethal dose…a body count those two old spinsters easily could've provided.

Thallium

Often referred to as "the poisoner's poison," human beings ingest small amounts of thallium in food, accumulating an average of .5 mg in the skeletal system and other bodily tissues. That small amount isn't toxic, but greater amounts can cause hair loss, exhaustion, numbness of the extremities, verbal impairment, and sleeplessness.

Thallium can fatally attack the central nervous system, particularly the heart. Once used in medicine to cure ringworm, thallium compounds are now restricted in most procedures, even banned as an ingredient in rat poison.

Thallium poisoning was depicted in Agatha Christie's mystery novel *The Pale Horse* (1961), which later informed some real-life investigations: a Latin American woman who was being slowly poisoned by her husband, a nurse treating a 19-month old child suffering from a mystery illness, and a doctor assisting a Scotland Yard investigation of mass murderer Graham Frederick Young all credit Christie's book for helping them solve their thallium mysteries.

Aluminum

The human body contains 60 mg of aluminum. Though not typically used as a poison, aluminum could prove toxic in the right amount.

Consider Buddy Ebsen's bum luck: originally cast as the Tin Man in *The Wizard of Oz* (1939), the actor began experiencing respiratory problems shortly after filming began due to an allergic reaction to the aluminum powder in his silver make-up. Ebsen's singing voice can still be heard briefly on the soundtrack, but his prolonged hospitalization was a boon for Jack Haley, who was recast as the Tin Man in one of the most celebrated films in motion picture history.

But don't pity Mr. Ebsen. He later struck "black gold" with *The Beverly Hillbillies,* playing a mountaineer who moves his family to California after discovering oil. "Texas tea" sat better with Buddy than silver face paint.

Chapter Nine
Necrophilia

Henri Blot was arrested in 1886 after he broke into a Parisian cemetery, disinterred the body of a recently deceased ballerina and proceeded to copulate with it. He fell asleep afterward, which resulted in his capture. At his trial he explained his perversion thusly, “Every man has his own taste. Mine is for corpses.” This begs the question: how do you get *that* taste out of your mouth?

Stories of undead sex abound in ancient and modern history, including recent examples set by notorious serial killers like Ed Gein, Ted Bundy and Jeffrey Dahmer. But necrophiliacs need not commit murder to practice their peculiar obsession. In fact, most never kill anyone, instead preying upon bodies that are already dead.

By 2008 over 20 US states had drafted necrophilia laws to prosecute this rare crime. Not only does necrophilia violate the body of the unwilling (albeit deceased) victim, but also poses a health hazard since dead human bodies carry harmful bacteria.

But if these dangers still don’t deter you (and the author of this book hopes that anyone with this particular predilection is duly deterred), at least exercise some semblance of civility when committing your heinous act. Set the mood with candles, soft lighting and tender music, because romance never dies, even if your partner does.

Till Death Do Us Part?

Use #35: Sex with the Dead

Necrophilia was so unfamiliar to Americans in the early 20th century that the first widely publicized scandal actually inspired public sympathy. Karl Tanzler von Cosel was a con artist, but his lurid affair with a dead person, and the strange affection the public felt toward him, was real.

Von Cosel, who called himself a Count, immigrated from Germany in 1930. He spun fantastical stories about his royal ancestry and bragged about his numerous science and medical degrees. In truth, he had a modest background and possessed no formal training, but his knowledge of mechanics helped him land a job as an X-ray technician at a Florida hospital. Soon he was regarded as a doctor and entrusted with the care of terminally ill patients.

He began treating Elena Hoyas Mesa, a 19-year old beauty suffering from tuberculosis. The courtly, 63-year old Von Cosel showered the girl and her family with presents, doted on her like an attentive lover, and administered phony medical treatments that nonetheless managed to revive the near-comatose woman a few times. Though their relationship remained platonic during her natural life, Von Cosel romanced her and repeatedly pressed her to marry him.

Elena died on Halloween night, 1931. Von Cosel struck a deal with Elena's father to inter her body in an above-ground mausoleum at von Cosel's expense. He then secretly returned to the mausoleum late at night, spending hours playing phonograph records beside his dead obsession. After six months he outfitted the door of the mausoleum with padlocks to ensure no one would enter the empty crypt, then absconded in a waiting taxi with Elena's petite, tightly wrapped body.

Von Cosel moved into a building that had once been a slaughterhouse and set up house, surrounded by his mechanical inventions, a wingless aircraft, and Elena Hoyas Mesa's quickly fading remains. Over the course of eight years he treated her body using homemade embalming methods, dressed her in a variety of outfits, and tried to preserve her once beautiful visage using an expensive germicidal antiseptic, makeup and paraffin wax. He laid her body in his bedroom and outfitted her with a gold wristwatch around her finger that served as a makeshift wedding ring.

Von Cosel believed he could bring Elena back to life. He employed a variety of mechanical means, including ultraviolet light and electrical currents to revive the long-deceased woman. As her body deteriorated he used wire to bind her fingers to her hands and her hands to her arms. He finally made the mistake of showing Elena to a curious couple, even demonstrating his technique of reviving her using electricity.

Word of von Cosel's experiments traveled to Elena's sister, who visited von Cosel with a Justice of the Peace. Hardly reticent, the old man proudly ushered them into his sleeping quarters. Her sister screamed when von Cosel raised the cloth covering Elena's grayish-white feet. She screamed again when he removed the entire cloth, exposing Elena's emaciated, rouge-colored face and manicured nails. "I beg you to leave her to me," von Cosel gently implored. "See how pretty she looks."

His appeal didn't work, and he was soon taken into custody. To this day, necrophilia is such a rare occurrence that many jurisdictions don't have laws on their books forbidding it, so local officials only charged him with grave robbing and set his bail at $1,000. Word spread of the hopeless romantic who couldn't bear to part from his true love, even in death, an indication that the public couldn't possibly grasp the full implications of von Cosel's actions. His newfound celebrity led to his quick release.

Von Cosel's admirers suggested placing Elena in a glass box for permanent display, thought not everyone was impressed by his unusual obsession. Von Cosel's estranged first wife explained to the press why their marriage didn't last: "I divorced him because, before we had sex, he wanted to put all this white wax makeup on me and for me to try not to breathe hard and to play dead."

After a brief period of public display, Elena's body was reburied in the dead of night so that von Cosel would not find her. Von Cosel later charged visitors 25 cents to tour the "love nest" that once housed Elena's body before he finally left town, setting up shop outside of Tampa where he sold postcards of Elena to passing tourists. After his death in 1952, a life-sized wax replica of Elena was found in his home. As the saying goes, true love never dies.

Public opinion towards necrophilia has changed as knowledge of its lurid nature has grown. Dalhousie University professors Peter Clark and Anthony Davis conducted a study in 1987 to measure what repulses people the most. Human tears rated low on the disgust meter, though anything involving sex and personal hygiene rated high. On a scale of one to five, men rated necrophilia a 4.6 while women rated it a solid 5.0.

In October 1993, 23-year old Ronald Shawn Ryan was sentenced to 10 years in prison for breaking into a funeral home twice and sexually assaulting the bodies of four elderly women. Employees noticed three of the bodies disturbed after the first break-in. Ryan assaulted the fourth body in its viewing room casket during the second break-in.

Ryan was convicted of two counts of burglary and one count of first degree malicious mischief. The sentencing judge urged lawmakers to properly criminalize necrophilia, stating, "This just shocks the conscience of this court and, I think, this community…this goes against the basic mores of our civilization."

In yet another act of burglary, 24-year old Phares Gonzalez and 23-year old Brandon Christopher were arrested after they broke into the mortuary at Forest Lawn Memorial-Park, Hollywood Hills, California.

The two men allegedly performed sexual acts with two corpses, one a 45-year old woman in a casket, the other a 75-year old woman found in the preparation area, though the two men claimed they only entered the mortuary to contact the dead using a Ouija board. Since there was no law in California against it at the time, the two men were not charged with necrophilia.

In 1989 Dr. Jonathan Rosman and Dr. Phillip Resnick reviewed 122 cases of necrophilic behavior and classified necrophiliacs into three basic categories:

Necrophilic homicide--the suspect commits murder in order to obtain a corpse.

Regular necrophilia--an already dead body is obtained for sexual gratification.

Necrophilic Fantasy--imagining the deed but not performing it.

In their findings, most necrophiliacs fit into the second category, and more than half of those subjects worked in a morgue or some other branch of the funeral business.

John Camden Bibbee, a former employee of United Pathology Laboratory, entered a plea agreement in 2002 to a charge of attempted necrophilia. He was discovered taking nude photos of a 17-year old Hispanic girl who had been shot to death.

Bibbee had previously assisted the Cochise County medical examiner during autopsies, which allowed him access to the young woman's body. He was caught when the photographs were found and his hand, which has an identifying scar, was seen in one of the pictures.

Also according to Dr. Rosman and Dr. Resnick, the most common motivation for necrophilia is to possess a compliant, nonresistant partner. The necrophiliac typically suffers from low self-esteem, fears rejection, is afraid of dead bodies (and thereby transforms his fear into desire), and constructs an elaborate fantasy involving sex with a corpse. Because necrophilia is so rare, and no single doctor has treated enough of them, an effective form of treatment hasn't been developed.

Not all necrophiliacs work near dead bodies, some just happen upon them. Consider Parker Clayton Ward, age 54 at the time of his arrest. He was asked to check up on a 43-year old woman in her camper. When she failed to answer, Ward telephoned her boyfriend, who instructed him to break down the door. Inside he found the unresponsive woman beside several empty pill bottles.

"I checked her pulse, then tried to give her mouth-to-mouth." Ward's voice grew soft as he described his crime to the court. "I knew it was kind of wrong…" When the judge asked him what he did next, Ward confessed, "I tried to have sex with her." Upon further questioning, Ward admitted that he did more than just "try."

"I had been drinking…I was pretty much drunk," Ward offered as his explanation. "No one can be that drunk," said the district attorney. He was charged with necrophilia and sentenced to four years in prison.

Scandal has often surrounded The Hells Angels, the legendary biker organization formed by restless WWII servicemen. Riots, accusations of drug trafficking, and general brutality have come to define the international motorcycle club, which helps fuel the rumor that the group's secret initiation ceremony involves acts of animal abuse, rape, and even necrophilia. True or not, the organization does itself no favors with its motto, "Three can keep a secret if two are dead."

In July, 2008, the state supreme court of Wisconsin ruled that existing state law does ban sex with a dead body, thereby bringing charges against three men who plundered a gravesite attempting to violate a corpse.

Twin brothers Nicholas and Alexander Grunke and their friend Dustin Radke, all 22-years old at the time charges were filed, entered a graveyard with shovels, a crowbar and a box of condoms. Nicholas had seen an obituary photo of a 20-year old woman who had recently died in a motorcycle accident and asked the other two to help him dig her up.

They managed to reach the coffin but were unable to open the concrete vault before a passing car scared them away, which eventually led to their capture. Each was convicted for their involvement and received prison terms.

Despite the growing number of states that have formally criminalized necrophilia, it's still considered by many to be a mental health issue that requires treatment rather than punishment. That was the conclusion in the case of Anthony Merino, a 24-year old semi-pro athlete who was caught having sex with the body of a 92-year old woman.

Merino was working as a lab technician at Holy Name Hospital in Teaneck, New Jersey when he snuck into the morgue late one night. A security guard found him after he had unzipped the woman's body bag and commenced the sexual assault. He reportedly used a latex glove as a condom.

He was charged with desecrating a human

corpse and convicted to seven years in prison, though he received time served through a plea bargain that also called for therapy. Under the deal he could never again work at a hospital, morgue, cemetery or funeral home. Just as well, considering the awful big blot on his resume.

Chapter Ten
Biological War Weapons

"War would end if the dead could return."

Stanley Baldwin
British Prime Minister,
1923-24, 1924-29, 1935-37

Casualties are common in war, so it's not surprising that military leaders throughout history have found creative ways to use dead human bodies in battle. Whether drawing toxic power from the dead, using them as missiles and bombs, or mining a dead body for elements of mass destruction, it's an unfortunate fact that a dead man can be just as lethal as a live one.

Poisoned Pointy Projectiles

Use #36: Scythian Arrow Heads

The Scythian civilization reigned over much of Central Asia between 600 BC and 300 AD. A nomadic, horse-riding culture, the Scythians were revered and feared for their battle expertise, particularly for the accuracy of their equestrian archers.

The Scythians beat back the Persian Army of King Darius I, fought alongside the Athenians in the Fifth Century BC, and later defeated a large army led by Alexander the Great. Scythian archers outmaneuvered their enemies by using hit and run attacks on horseback. They also carried hundreds of arrows into battle in specially designed cases that separated the arrows between different arrow points and, more importantly, different toxins.

Adversaries could expect an agonizing death if struck with a barbed or double tipped Scythian arrow, since the Scythians were known to dip their arrow heads in the blood of decomposing human bodies, causing death by tetanus or gangrene. After the onset of delirium, a victim would usually succumb to bacterial infection within days, or suffer lifelong paralysis and constant infection if he managed to survive the attack.

In Greek Fire, Poison Arrows, and Scorpion Bombs, author Adrienne Mayor described a more elaborate form of Scythian arrow toxin: Scythicon, an elaborate mixture of human blood, snake venom, and human or animal feces.

Carried in specially designed vials attached to the archers belt buckles, the bacteria-festooned Scythicon could cause death in a multitude of ways. The vials masked the atrocious smell of putrefied blood, venom and feces, a potent stench which served as an early form of psychological warfare, too.

Scythian Facts

Scythians were rumored to fashion quivers from human arms and drink from the gilded skulls of their fallen enemies...probably not the wisest move, if their enemy was felled by a poisoned arrow. That'd be one noxious beverage.

Don't Drink the Water
Use #37: Poisoned Water Supplies

Water is an essential part of any community. Settlements, towns, and cities are built around reliable sources of water, so poisoning a water supply can often prove fatal.

The ancient Greeks popularized this tactic when they began polluting their enemy's water supplies with dead animal carcasses around 300 BC. The Romans and the Persians used this strategy, too, followed by the Iroquois Indians centuries later during their war with the French in 1710.

German emperor Frederick Barbarossa provides

one of the most notorious examples of this practice. Angered by the residents of Tortona, who refused to accept his sovereignty and allied themselves with his enemies, Barbarossa launched an assault against the Italian city in 1155 AD.

As chronicled in *The Deeds of Frederick Barbarossa* by his uncle, Otto of Freisling, Barbarossa was repelled by the city's fortified walls and natural barriers. After failing to conquer the city using traditional means of assault, Barbarossa's army resorted to poisoning the city's water supply--a nearby spring--with the dead bodies of Tortona's fallen warriors.

As Otto of Freisling wrote, Barbarossa wished "to constrain by lack of drinking water those who were hedged in by nature's defenses, proceeded to make the aforementioned spring useless for human needs. There were thrown into it the rotting and putrid corpses of men and beasts." No one in the 12th century knew that dead human bodies carried deadly bacteria, but it's a sure bet the people of Tortona knew that floating corpses in their water supply was not a good thing.

According to his biography, the people of Tortona delivered an impassioned plea for mercy, threw themselves at Barbarossa's feet, and delivered the emperor a resounding victory. Of course, when your uncle is also your biographer, it's easy to claim just about anything.

Bubonic Bombs
Use #38: Catapult Fodder

Pity the poor guy living in the Middle Ages who had to contend with the era's many hardships: the feudal system, the bubonic plague, and falling dead bodies launched by giant catapults.

The catapult was the most effective weapon of mass destruction during the middle ages, a device that reached its zenith with the creation of the trebuchet. Faster and more accurate than standard catapults, the trebuchet used a lever attached to a sturdy wooden frame that launched its cargo in an arc by using a heavy counterweight. The trebuchet could lob heavy stones hundreds of feet, demolishing fortified castle walls.

In addition to huge rocks, the trebuchet was loaded with an assortment of ammunition to cripple or hamper an enemy's defenses: Greek Fire (flaming wooden barrels that exploded upon contact), animal body parts, feces, and dead human bodies, both intact and in pieces.

The most common human catapult fodder were fallen soldiers, or messengers sent to deliver terms and conditions which obviously weren't received well. Sometimes severed heads or stray body parts were launched in place of entire bodies, depending on the size of the trebuchet, availability of ammunition, or temperament of the catapult operator.

The most effective man missiles were those

killed by the bubonic plague. Also known as the Black Death, the plague killed an estimated one quarter to two thirds of Europe's population, with an estimated worldwide death toll of 75 million. A highly infectious bacterial disease, the sickness proved fatal within days and remained contagious long after the victim died.

Launching plague-infested dead bodies over castle walls had a dual effect. The impact of a dead body landing on an individual would likely prove lethal to the unsuspecting target, while the splattered remains would fester in the unsanitary fortress interior. The entire population of a castle could be wiped out within days.

Modern Day Applications

For the armchair warrior who dreams wistfully of times past when a man could lay siege to an entire city and decimate everyone in his path, take heart. With a little creativity and a good deal of ingenuity, you could build your own catapult, too.

Plus, if one of your relatives dies and you can't afford a proper burial, why not send your loved one into the great beyond by literally sending your loved one into the great beyond? This would have the added benefit of exacting revenge against a neighbor who plays loud music or parks an unregistered car in his front yard. Don't be discouraged, the construction materials aren't as primitive as you think…

In *Adventures from the Technology Underground*, intrepid author William Gurstelle describes the modern gladiators who build medieval weapons for their personal recreation. Armed with the proper schematics, today's catapult enthusiasts could build their own tossing machines and launch any number of ammo substitutes: pumpkins, lawn furniture, or, depending on local zoning laws, your late Uncle Lenny.

Catapult Facts

Examples abound of dead human body hurling throughout the Middle Ages. In 1422, Lithuanian forces in Carolstein launched a potent combo of dead human bodies and mass quantities of manure over the castle's walls in an apparently successful attempt to spread disease.

The Mongols were also believed to launch dead human bodies, particularly during their siege against the Genoese in Crimea during the 1340's.

Cold Comfort
Use #39: Contaminated Blankets

Smallpox is a highly contagious, often times fatal disease that first emerged in human populations thousands of years ago. The disease has been effectively eradicated, but it's estimated that hundreds of millions of people have died from smallpox throughout history. The Native American Indian population was particularly hard hit by smallpox after the arrival of the Europeans, who brought the disease to the New World.

An estimated 20 million Native Americans, up to 95% of the indigenous population, are believed to have died from smallpox. The disease acted as an unintentional biological weapon, though speculation exists that British forces intentionally spread the disease. Did the British give blankets used by smallpox victims to the Native American Indians?

Evidence suggests they at least considered the idea. In a series of letters concerning the siege of Fort Pitt during the French-Indian War (in which opposing French and British forces allied with separate Indian tribes), British General Jeffrey Amherst wrote to Colonel Henry Bouquet, "Could it not be contrived to send smallpox among the disaffected tribes of Indians?"

Bouquet responded, "I will try to inoculate the bastards with some blankets that may fall into their hands, and take care not to get the disease myself." The garments and bed sheets used by smallpox victims were usually sterilized or destroyed to halt the spread of the disease, so blankets used by smallpox victims could've easily infected the Indian population who used them.

Amherst responded to Bouquet, "You will do well to inoculate the Indians by means of blankets, as well as every other method that can serve to extirpate this execrable race." Scholars differ on whether this dastardly deed was carried out, though it is true the Native American forces were severely crippled by an outbreak of smallpox. It's also true that Captain Simeon Ecuyer, during a discussion with the Indians at Fort Pitt, gave his enemies a handkerchief and two blankets that were exposed to smallpox.

It's impossible to know if the offending handkerchief and blankets had the intended effect, or if the disease had already taken hold of the Indian tribe, but the smallpox outbreak did help the British route their besiegers and save Fort Pitt. As for the blankets, smallpox on clothing and similar materials can remain contagious for many years. That's a potent and long-lasting biological weapon, one for which there is no actual cure, though the smallpox vaccine did stamp out the disease by the 1970's.

Smallpox Fact

According to the Centers for Disease Control and Prevention, smallpox can be transmitted by face to face contact, exposure to infected bodily fluids, or contact with contaminated clothing or bedding.

Foggy Field of Battle
Use #40: Chlorine Gas Attack

Chemical weapons, like much of current warfare, were ushered into the modern era during World War I.

German forces advancing on Ypres, France used canisters to disperse chlorine gas while fighting entrenched French and Algerian forces. After strategically placing 5,730 cylinders in advance of the battle, the Germans opened the canisters when the wind proved favorable and spread the poisonous gas across the battlefield.

Chlorine gas acts as a pulmonary irritant on the respiratory system. A greenish-yellow gas heavier than air, it burns the eyes and causes blindness, induces coughing and nausea as it scorches the airways, and prompts a feeling of drowning as the lungs fill with fluid.

Unaware of the impending danger, the French and Algerian troops watched as the chlorine gas moved slowly in their direction, believing that the smoke cloud masked an advancing army. They dug in and prepared for battle until the cloud swept over them and wrought a paralyzing, disorienting effect that broke a hole in their defenses, which the advancing Germans exploited.

The Bottom Line

Chlorine is a common element found in the human body, to the tune of 95 grams in the average person. The Germans released a total of 1,600 large and 4,130 small steel chlorine canisters, for a total of 160 metric tons of chlorine. That averages about 28,000 grams of chlorine per canister. The chlorine contents of about 295 dead human bodies could produce one German WWI chlorine canister.

Over six hundred French and Algerian troops died as a result of that attack. The combined chlorine contents of those 600 bodies totaled 57,000 grams, so the chlorine contents of those fallen soldiers could've provided the chlorine needed for two chlorine canisters.

The chlorine contents of 1,684,219 dead human bodies could've provided enough chlorine for all of the canisters used in that attack. A nearly prophetic number, given that the total WWI deaths in France alone totaled 1,897,800.

Do-It-Yourself

If you enjoy World War I re-enactments (or if you just like to blow stuff up), there are a variety of homemade, low-intensity chlorine bomb recipes.

The ingredients can be found in most households, with the main ingredient being three or four chlorine tablets…or the chlorine contents of 7-9 dead human bodies.

Suffice it to say, it's important to mix the ingredients quickly and run away from the impending explosion, so only trained professionals or fatalistic morons are advised to try.

Chapter 11
Psychological Warfare

"One death is a tragedy, a million deaths a statistic."

attributed to Joseph Stalin
Soviet Dictator

Perception means a lot, especially in war. This is proven by the following ways in which dead human bodies have been used to wage psychological battle.

The Mongol Threat
Use #41: Propaganda Cannibalism

Genghis Khan and his descendents struck terror in the hearts of their enemies, decimated entire cities and killed tens of millions of people. The Mongols were so feared that Europeans attributed them with beastly behavior, particularly cannibalism.

In *Consuming Passions*, author Merrall Llewelyn Price recounts a passage from the 1248 publication *Historia Tartarorum* in which the Mongols "devour human flesh like lions." An earlier account, *Chronica Majora* by Matthew Paris, describes the Mongol cannibals as consuming old and ugly women while sexually assaulting younger women until they died from exhaustion--then eating them, too.

That's hardly the stuff upstanding reputations are built on, and European propagandists knew it. Harsh rhetoric was meant to rally complacent Europeans to dizzying heights of paranoia and self-defense. In truth, the Mongols were merely the latest to be characterized by this type of propaganda, a tradition that was also directed at the Scythians and Huns.

The smear campaign was unnecessary, since internal power struggles and splintering territories finally brought down the Mongol Empire. Meanwhile, the Europeans are still waiting to be eaten. Better luck next time.

Mongol Facts

The Mongol territories of the 13th century stretched from modern day Hungary to Korea and from Siberia to Tibet, the largest contiguous empire in world history.

Despite their reputation, the Mongols ruled their subjects with surprising tolerance and innovation. They established reasonable codes of law, secured safe trade routes, preached religious tolerance, and even oversaw a reliable postal system.

Richard Not-for-the-Fainthearted
Use #42: Crusading Cannibals

The Crusades spawned many legends, half-truths, and fabrications that persist to this day.

A popular poem about King Richard the Lionhearted claimed that he was nursed back to health by eating human meat. Richard fell sick during his military campaign and asked his men for pork, which he believed would cure his illness. Pork was hard to come by in the Muslim world, so Richard's men fed him the flesh of an enemy Saracen under the guise of pig meat.

Richard was told the truth after he recovered and was thrilled by the deception, so he invited the Saracens to a banquet, not telling his guests that the main course would be dead prisoners-of-war. The Saracen representatives took flight when Richard began carving the head of a Saracen warrior.

This light-hearted depiction of anthropophagy, written centuries after his military campaign ended, played upon Richard's brutish image and served to dehumanize his Muslim opponents (thus the pork-like taste of their flesh). It also highlights Richard's knack for psychological warfare, since the Saracen representatives flee in disgust and word spreads of the Western aggressors frightening tactics.

But not every story of Crusade cannibalism worked in favor of the accused, such as the Frankish Army's rumored cannibalism. The rumors appalled their enemies, but also inspired disgust and anti-war sentiments at home, prompting the Franks to reconsider their military participation in the Crusades.

Most of these stories are dubious, some are outright folklore. War propaganda is as much a product of passion and conjecture than actual fact. These stories, like a good piece of meat, should be taken with a grain of salt.

Crusade Facts

The Crusades were nine separate military campaigns between 1095 and 1272, launched by Europeans in an effort to recapture Jerusalem and stop Muslim expansion.

Anthropophagy is the clinical term for noshing on humans.

The Franks were Germanic people who dominated Western Europe for centuries.

Chapter 12
Weapons of Combustion

"Why build, knowing destruction is inevitable?
Why yearn life, knowing all things must die?"

Franz Kafka

If you've ever been called self-destructive, take heart--we all are. The human body contains elements that, when properly combined, can cause serious destruction.

Ka-Boom!
Use #43: Gunpowder

Merchants along the Silk Road traded gunpowder for hundreds of years before it's potential was discovered by merchants of war. What was once a playful noise maker soon became the most destructive force known to the old world.

Gunpowder clouded the battlefields of Europe, blasted the mounted knight into obscurity and decimated the catapult. Black powder burned its way into Mongol and Chinese skirmishes, prompting redesigned defenses and new methods of attack. New World natives were quickly subdued by European conquerors who possessed it's awful explosive power.

Gunpowder played a central role in warfare for hundreds of years. Not bad for an otherwise simple concoction of common ingredients: potassium nitrate (also known as saltpeter), charcoal and sulfur.

The Bottom Line

All of the makings for gunpowder can be found in the human body (potassium, nitrogen, oxygen, carbon and sulfur). A common formula for creating gunpowder involves mixing potassium nitrate, charcoal and sulfur in a ratio of 15:3:2, respectively.

The combined ingredients in one dead human body could produce about 12 ounces of gunpowder. Ever been told you have an explosive personality? Now you know why.

Gunpowder Facts

Other names for gunpowder include fire drug, fire-chemical, black powder, smokeless powder, smoke balls, and serpentine.

Gunpowder was likely developed by Chinese alchemists in the ninth or tenth century; it's first application remains it's most common use today--a noise maker in fireworks.

Gunpowder's use in warfare was supplanted in the 19th century when Alfred Nobel created nitroglycerin.

Ka-Boom, Too!
Use #44: Blasting Caps

Blasting caps are used to detonate highly powerful, hard-to-handle explosives. A blasting cap is a cylinder closed at one side and open at the other to allow a detonating mechanism to be inserted, such as a fuse.

Inside the blasting cap is an igniter mix that sets off the primary explosive at the center of the cap, which in turn detonates the final combustible at the base. This final detonation triggers the main explosive attached to the blasting cap, such as dynamite.

Tetryl is a volatile explosive compound once commonly used in blasting caps. It's not found in nature, but rather manufactured using a combination of other compounds. The human body contains the raw materials to make over 12 pounds of tetryl.

If That Doesn't Spark Your Interest

Gunpowder was once used to make blasting caps, too. The first primitive blasting cap was used in 1745 when Dr. Watson of the British Royal Society used an electric spark from a Leyden jar to explode black powder.

Blasting Cap Facts

Benjamin Franklin developed a commercial blasting cap consisting of a paper tube filled with black powder, ignited by a large electric spark from two wires.

Alfred Nobel created a blasting cap for dynamite employing mercury fulminate.

Other materials used to create blasting caps include sodium azide, lead azide, and tellurium.

Little Boy's Big Impact
Use #45: Atomic Bomb

The Manhattan Project was launched during World War II to create the world's first atomic weapon.

It was the result of decades of scientific research and a years-long battle between the Nazis and Allied forces that saw millions of people killed and much of Europe scorched by heavy, constant artillery.

German scientists managed to split the atom in 1938 through a process called nuclear fission, which releases tremendous amounts of energy in the form of heat and radiation. This pressured European and American scientists to uncover the secrets of atomic energy and build a bomb first. One major obstacle was finding enough enriched uranium, the primary fuel for an atomic bomb, so intense efforts were launched to find vast amounts of uranium ore and extract the rare material.

The arms race ultimately favored the Allied Powers. Two atomic bombs, the uranium-powered "Little Boy" and the plutonium-powered "Fat Man," were dropped by American forces on Hiroshima and Nagasaki, Japan, in 1945. The catastrophic destruction brought the second world war to a decisive end but afterwards launched a dangerous, atomic-fueled "Cold War" that lasted for many decades.

The Bottom Line

The scientists who worked on the Manhattan Project went to great lengths to secure quality uranium for "Little Boy," amounting to 64.1 kilograms of highly enriched uranium. The human body contains a small amount of uranium, about 0.1 milligrams.

Only a small portion of the 0.1 mg. of uranium

in the human body is usable in an atomic bomb, requiring the contributions of billions of dead human bodies to make just one "Little Boy." Which is just as well, since the awesome power of atomic weaponry shouldn't be in the hands of just one person.

Casualties of War

Use #46: Human Bombs in Iraq

IEDs--improvised explosive devices--were a common threat faced by coalition forces during the Iraq War. Often found along roadsides, IEDs are crude, homemade bombs of varying potency. Some IEDs are designed to distract coalition forces from another, larger attack, while other IEDs inflict severe damage on soldiers, civilians and surrounding structures.

Most IEDs are made of simple materials: an explosive charge, a detonation device, and an apparatus that sets off the charge. They might also contain shrapnel that bursts upon detonation. The loose definition of an IED could apply to any number of incendiary devices used in conflicts throughout history.

Troops commonly found human remains littered across the Iraqi landscape. This posed a special problem since enemy combatants took to hiding IEDs in or around dead human bodies. Coalition forces, Iraqi police and civilians who came upon these corpses were often killed or wounded when the bodies exploded, sometimes with enough force to cripple armored vehicles and decimate entire crowds of people.

When it comes to inflicting death, human beings know few limits. When it comes to returning the favor, neither do the dead.

Chapter 13
Sources of Power

Some people refuse to take death lying down. Take Angel Pantoja Medina, a young Puerto Rican man whose dying wish was to be propped up on his feet during his funeral wake. Wearing a baseball cap and sunglasses, Medina's lifeless body stood for three days in his mother's living room thanks to a special embalming method. His brother Carlos explained Medina's unusual last request thusly: "He wanted to be happy, standing."

Standing for three days straight requires an awful lot of stamina, so it's not surprising that a dead human body contains the goods to produce many sources of energy.

Power to the Dead People
Use #47: Batteries

Like two lovers meeting in the night, a pair of electrodes combine to form a chemical reaction. When joined by an electrolyte, the chemical reaction generates electricity and forms the device commonly known as a battery.

A variety of metals and metallic compounds can serve as positive and negative electrodes. When a negative and a positive are joined by an electrolyte (acid or salt mixture), the chemical reaction generates an electrical current that can power a wide variety of machines.

Some materials power the inexpensive batteries used in flashlights and alarm clocks, while more potent, costlier materials power the tiny batteries used in hearing aids and watches. Many ingredients can be used to create electrodes and electrolytes, including coins, lemons…and one dead human body.

The human body contains many of the ingredients used to build batteries. For example, the 2.3 grams of zinc in one dead human body could provide the zinc content for one AAA-alkaline battery.

The 120 mg of lead in one dead human body could provide the lead content for 120 AA-alkaline batteries, or 60 C-alkaline batteries. Zinc-carbon batteries also contain lead--one dead human body could provide the lead content for seven AA zinc-carbon batteries.

The cadmium content of 194 dead human bodies could provide the cadmium content for one C nickel-cadmium battery, while 240 dead human bodies could supply one D-battery. That's nothing compared to the nickel content of one C nickel-cadmium battery, requiring the nickel contributions of over one thousand dead human bodies.

The average lithium battery requires the lithium contributions of 139 dead human bodies. Lithium batteries are often used in pacemakers and other devices requiring long life, which is exactly what you hope for in a battery…and a human body.

When You Need Something More Potent than a 9-Volt

Use #48: Thorium Fuel

When it came time to name the new element he discovered in 1828, Swedish chemist Jons Jakob Berzelius reached back to Norse mythology and selected Thor, the powerful thunder God who could summon lightning bolts from his fingertips. Berzelius must have felt like he was handling lightning, too, when he discovered Thorium, though its full potential wouldn't be realized for another century.

The isotope thorium-232 is used in the production of nuclear fuel. While the 0.1 milligrams of thorium in the human body is a very small amount, all the thorium mined throughout the world has the potential to serve as nuclear fuel.

According to the World Nuclear Association, the AVR experimental pebble beach reactor in Julich, Germany (population 33,822) used 1,360 kg of thorium over a 21 year period, requiring the thorium contributions of billions of dead human bodies.

That calls for a serious baby boom among the good people of Julich, a tall order just to keep a nuclear reactor running. Seeing that Germany is the birthplace of Norse mythology, maybe they should summon Thor and his powerful lightning bolts instead.

I've Got the Wind at My Back

Use #49: Sailing Material

The Egyptians, Greeks and Phoenicians were among the first to construct sailboats about 4,000 years ago. Harnessing the power of wind by attaching a cloth to the mast of a ship spared slave laborers from having to propel large vessels across the ocean using wooden oars. Sailing ships dominated naval activity for several centuries.

The earliest sails were constructed out of animal skin. As luck would have it, human skin can be tanned to approximate the look and feel of animal hide. Maximized to its fullest potential, one dead human body could produce an 18-square foot sail.

That much human skin could construct a riding sail, which helps vessels maintain control in strong winds and avoid ship damage. Or you could just attach your skin-sail to any small boat and sail off into the sunset--much like the dead guy who provided your sail.

Body Burning
Use #50: Locomotive Fuel

"Even popularity can be overdone," Mark Twain once wrote. He could've been referring to himself. Widely known as a humorist during his lifetime, history has enhanced Twain's reputation and given credibility to comments he probably didn't mean seriously.

In his travelogue *The Innocents Abroad*, Twain discussed the many things he overheard during his aborted trip to the Middle East, including this interlude about train travel: "I shall not speak of the railway, for it is unlike any other railway--I shall only say that the fuel used for the locomotive is composed of mummies three thousand years old, purchased by the ton or by the graveyard for that purpose."

He goes on to say about the inefficient fuel source, "sometimes one hears the profane engineer call out pettishly, 'D--m these plebeians (commoners), they don't burn worth a cent--pass out a King.'" Twain's reputation, and the fact that traditional locomotive fuel like wood and coal were scarce in Egypt, has firmly established this claim, which has since been reported by the British Broadcasting Company and published in *Discover* Magazine.

Using mummified human remains to power a locomotive is not entirely out of the question. Wood and coal produce carbon when burned, and a dead human body is composed of 16 kilograms of carbon.

But anyone who gives Twain's words more weight than they deserve need only read the author's footnote: "Stated to me for a fact. I only tell it as I got it. I am willing to believe it. I can believe any thing." That's hardly an endorsement, though it's more believable than some of the other wild claims he made in the book.

True or not, Twain probably wouldn't mind the attention he still receives. As the man himself also said, "It's better to be popular than right."

It's a Gas, Gas, Gas
Use #51: Gasoline

True or not, burning Egyptian mummies for fuel is not a practical source of energy. And besides, when's the last time you rode on a steam engine?

Automobiles have long since displaced locomotives as our main mode of transportation, and a car's primary energy source is gasoline. Fossil fuels, from which gasoline is derived, are the fossilized remains of dead plants and animals formed in the Earth's crust over millions of years.

Human beings haven't walked the Earth that long, but in 100 million years our dead human bodies could serve as fuel for the next generation of gas-guzzlers. If you lack the patience to wait, there are other ways a dead human body could top off your tank.

The manganese compound MMT is added to unleaded gasoline to boost its octane rating. One dead human body contains 12 milligrams of manganese. Likewise, samarium is used in the production of ethanol, an alternative fuel source derived from corn. One dead human body also contains 50 micrograms of samarium.

Manpower
Use #52: Alternative Car Fuels

Rising gas prices have motorists screaming for alternative fuels. Air, hydrogen and water are excellent sources of energy, as our own bodies can attest.

Zero Pollution Motors has developed a low-cost automobile powered by air. The technology uses compressed air in place of traditional gasoline combustion to fire the car's engine pistons, while the motor can be plugged in to refill the air tank when it's not in use. Many water-powered engine prototypes also exist, some of which can be found on the internet. A water-powered automobile fires an electric motor by harnessing the energy that chemically bonds hydrogen and oxygen atoms, the elements that make water.

You can bolster your environmental credentials by recycling the 12 gallons of water in one dead human body for use in your water-powered roadster. If you opt for an air-powered car, keep in mind that the air we breathe is 78% nitrogen, 21% oxygen and 1% a variety of lesser gases. One dead human body contains 1.3 kg of nitrogen, 43 kg of oxygen, and a host of lesser gases.

Chapter 14
Scientific Measurements

Determined to prove that lightning was a form of electricity, Benjamin Franklin and his son flew a kite with a key attached during a thunderstorm. As lightning struck the kite, sparks of electricity shot from the key and onto Franklin's hand, giving the legendary statesman an electrical shock.

Franklin was lucky to escape with a superficial injury. Hundreds of people are injured by lightning every year, and dozens die as a result. Losing one's life is a high price to pay for a weather experiment, though it should be noted that, in case of death, one dead human body could provide the resources to conduct weather, electrical, and many other types of scientific research.

That would've thrilled Franklin, the most famous inventor of his day. If equipped with today's scientific knowledge, there's no telling how he would've put *us* to good use.

RIP

I Was Abducted by a Weather Balloon

Use #53: Hydrogen-Filled Weather Balloons

Due to their unusual shape, strange movement in the sky, and wishful thinking on the part of sci-fi geeks, weather balloons are sometimes mistaken for extraterrestrial UFO's. Meteorology may not hold the same fascination as alien pod people embedded in meteorites, but weather balloons do serve an important, earthly purpose.

The four key measurements taken in meteorology (temperature, pressure, humidity, and wind speed) are all used to forecast future weather patterns. Notwithstanding weather satellites and other cutting edge technologies, much of modern forecasting still relies on manually operated weather balloons and the use of a radiosonde, a device that measures temperature, barometric pressure, and moisture. Radiosondes are attached to weather balloons, then raised at a rate of about 1,000 feet per minute to measure atmospheric conditions at different altitudes. The movement of the balloon is also monitored by a radar to measure wind speed.

But a weather balloon is little more than a lump of latex with a dream without the aid of hydrogen, which is used to inflate the large, globe-shaped instruments. The amount of hydrogen required to inflate a weather balloon depends on the size of the balloon, current atmospheric pressure and the expected final altitude of the balloon, which will expand under pressure as it climbs higher into the sky.

If we assume 775 liters of hydrogen gas needed for one balloon, the 7 kilograms of hydrogen in one dead human body could inflate about 100 weather balloons.

Weather surveys are taken twice daily from locations around the world. About 100 radiosonde-equipped weather balloons are launched in the U.S., so the hydrogen from one dead human body could launch all of those balloons one time.

About 800 weather balloons are launched worldwide, so eight dead human bodies could provide the needed hydrogen for one set of worldwide weather balloons, while 16 dead human bodies could provide the hydrogen for a full day's worth of weather forecasting around the globe.

Finally, if your local weatherman is guilty of bad predictions, you could fire off a letter to the American Meteorological Society (http://www.ametsoc.org/), which boasts a membership of over 11,000...which, coincidentally, could provide enough hydrogen for about two years of weather forecasting.

This begs the question: just how dedicated are members of the American Meteorological Society?

You Want Me to Stick It Where?
Use #54: Mercury Thermometers

Have you ever noticed how boiling water rises to the top of a pot? Water molecules speed up when heated and cause the hot liquid to bubble up, which is the principle behind a common bulb thermometer. As the temperature increases, the liquid in the bulb thermometer climbs up the temperature scale. Bulb thermometers can be used to measure both weather and human body temperatures.

Mercury is a common element used in thermometers because it has a lower freezing point and a higher boiling point than water, so it can be used in many different climates. Your body temperature will never fluctuate more than a few degrees during your lifetime, but mercury is useful in fever thermometers because it heats and cools quickly.

The six milligrams of mercury in the human body could be put to good use in a fever thermometer, which typically contain anywhere from 0.5 to three grams of mercury. The mercury content of about 167 dead human bodies could fill one thermometer containing one gram of mercury.

So remember, if you're hot under the collar, feeling a bit frigid, or if bad puns make your blood boil, measure your response in the spirit of your body's mercury content.

Not Hot Enough For You?

Gallium is sometimes used as a substitute for mercury in high temperature thermometers. Like mercury, gallium has a high melting point and is a liquid at room temperature, but it is significantly less toxic than mercury. The human body contains only 0.7 milligrams of gallium, so about 1,429 dead human bodies would be required to produce one gram of gallium.

Thermometer Facts

Galileo Galilei is famous for stating that the Earth revolves around the sun, but he was also a noted inventor who created an early thermometer in the late 16th century.

Daniel Fahrenheit developed a mercury-based thermometer with a standardized measuring scale. His scale states water's freezing point as 32 degrees and boiling point as 212 degrees.

Anders Celsius developed his self-named scale years after Fahrenheit, which states water's freezing point as 0 degrees and boiling point as 100 degrees.

A third temperature scale, Kelvin, is used mainly by scientists.

Mercury in thermometers has been gradually phased out and replaced with other materials that are not as dangerous.

The Weatherman's Been Under a lot of Pressure Lately
Use #55: Mercury Barometer

The air around us is made up of tiny molecules. Most of us breathe air at about sea level, so imagine those air molecules as if they were pieces of popcorn in a plastic bag. If the bag of popcorn is squeezed tightly the pieces will push together within a smaller amount of space, which is what happens to air molecules under high pressure. If the bag is stretched the popcorn will have more room, similar to air molecules under low pressure.

Meteorologists measure air pressure as a way to forecast short-term weather patterns. High pressure causes cooler temperatures and clear skies, while low pressure causes warm weather and rain by heating the water molecules in the air. Atmospheric pressure is measured using a device called a barometer.

A barometer resembles a large thermometer, and the similarities don't end there. Both instruments use a variety of liquids, most commonly mercury, to produce a measurement. High atmospheric pressure forces the mercury up the barometer, while low atmospheric pressure causes the mercury level to drop.

The size, shape, and age of a mercury barometer can affect its mercury content, but most contain around 100-600 grams of mercury. If we assume a mercury content of 300 grams, then 50,000 dead human bodies could provide the mercury content for one barometer.

Do These Air Molecules Make Me Look Fat?

Italian physicist Evangelista Torricelli wished to create an instrument that would measure the weight of air. He planned to use water instead of mercury, but water is not as dense as mercury, so he would've needed a lot water and a glass tube several feet high.

Will I Have to Work an Extra Hour 300 Million Years From Now?
Use #56: Atomic Clocks

Imagine hovering far above the Earth along the equator, seeing firsthand how half the world is cloaked in darkness while the other half is bathed in sunlight. This common phenomena produces the 24-hour day, and divides our time on Earth between weeks, months and years.

It's humbling to think of the Earth in such a simple, stark manner, and even more so to see it in action: visit www.time.gov and click on the interactive map to show the exact time in your region and where in the world the sun is currently shining. And take note of the actual time--it's the most accurate clock known to man.

That's because www.time.gov uses an atomic clock, a form of timekeeping more precise than the Earth's rotation, since the planet's speed of rotation changes over millions of years. For instance, a day on Earth 600 million years ago only lasted 22 hours, while an Earth day millions of years in the future will be longer. Satellites, space probes and other electronic transmissions depend on pinpoint precision to function properly, so atomic clocks have become the standard means of time keeping due to their constant, unwavering accuracy.

The element cesium is most often used to power atomic clocks, which gauge time by stimulating cesium at the atomic level and measuring the frequency it produces. Under the proper stimulation, cesium atoms will oscillate 9,192,631,770 times over a very short period of time, or what is known as an atomic second. The rate that cesium oscillates under the proper stimulation is constant, so the amount of time measured is constant, too.

One gram of cesium can power an atomic clock for over a year. Six milligrams of cesium can be found in the human body, so the cesium content of one dead human body could power an atomic clock for roughly two days. About 167 dead human bodies could keep an atomic clock ticking for a full year.

Who Can Turn the World On with a Smile? You, That's Who!

Use #57: LEDs

Now that you have a state-of-the-art method for determining time, you'll need a way to display it.

LEDs (light emitting diodes) are a popular source of light because they last much longer and produce more light per watt than traditional light bulbs.

LEDs can create visible, infrared and ultraviolet light depending on the materials used to create them, and are useful in many battery-powered devices such as digital clocks.

The construction materials used also determine the color of the LED. For example, aluminum gallium arsenide produces red and infrared light. The human body contains aluminum, gallium, and arsenic. When combined, one dead human body could produce 1.7 mg. of aluminum gallium arsenide.

Aluminum gallium phosphide creates green light, so the phosphorus in one dead human body combined with the aluminum and gallium could produce 1.27 mg. of aluminum gallium phosphide. If you'd like to create red-orange, orange, yellow or green light, the indium in one dead human body combined with the others could produce 825 micrograms of aluminum gallium indium phosphide.

The gallium and nitrogen in one dead human body could produce 837 micrograms of gallium nitride, which emits emerald green and blue light, while the 675.5 micrograms of potential indium gallium nitride from one dead human body would produce ultraviolet, bluish-green and blue light. Different LEDs can be combined to produce an array of colors, making the human body awash in a rainbow of possibilities.

Chapter 15
Materials and Components

"Life is pleasant. Death is peaceful. It's the transition that's troublesome."

Isaac Asimov

Asimov's novels inspired a generation of scientists, so it's fitting that his musings on death should inspire a chapter about the scientific materials found in a dead human body.

We Are Iron Men
Use #58: Cast Iron

After defeating the Tartars in 954 AD, Chinese Emperor Shih Tsung celebrated his victory by commissioning a 40-ton sculpture, the Great Lion of Tsang-chou, made entirely out of cast iron. It's unknown what enticed the Emperor more--lions, cast iron, or obscene acts of ego-stroking--but it is known that 40 tons of anything made out of cast iron was a tall order back in the 10th century.

That's because pure iron has a high melting point, requiring a level of heat not possible at that time. European metallurgists developed blast furnaces hot enough to do the job centuries later, but Chinese craftsmen began producing iron goods much earlier by burning iron ore mixed with charcoal, which produced an iron-carbon alloy that could be easily melted and cast into any number of implements.

Modern cast iron employs a number of additives to produce an alloy. One recipe listed on freepatentsonline.com includes these elements mixed in this composition:

Silicon: 58-70% (total weight of the alloy)
Calcium: 0.5-1.8%
Aluminum: 0.5-1.8%
Manganese: 2.5-7.0%
Zirconium: 1.0-7.0%
Cerium: 1.0-3.0%
Lanthanum: 0.5-1.5%

Iron: remainder

As luck and Mother Nature would have it, the human body contains all of those elements in these amounts:

Silicon: 1.0 gram
Calcium: 1.0 kilogram
Aluminum: 60 milligrams
Manganese: 12 milligrams
Zirconium: 1 milligram
Cerium: 40 milligrams
Lanthanum: 0.8 milligrams
Iron: 4.2 grams

If we mix the minimum amount of each additive (totaling 64% of the alloy) then add the remaining amount of iron (36%), one dead human body could produce 100 milligrams of cast iron.

That's not very much, since it would take 400 million dead human bodies to produce the Great Lion of Tsang-chou, though that should satisfy any emperor's blood lust...and ego.

You've Got a Magnetic Personality
Use #59: Magnets

Computers, electric motors and household appliances are just some of the miracles of innovation that employ magnets. A magnet can be made out of any number of substances, including metal, ceramics and plastic, each one possessing a north/south magnetic field created by electrons specially arranged at the atomic level. Magnets attract other materials that possess magnetic ability, thus allowing Wile. E Coyote to chase an iron pellet-fed roadrunner while wearing roller skates and a giant magnet.

Iron, cobalt and nickel are common magnetic metals, and each one can be found in the human body. The iron, cobalt and nickel in one dead human body add up to just over 4.2 grams of magnetic material.

If you're fascinated by both magnets and Looney Tunes cartoons, ACME International Inc. (www.aimcs.com) sells refrigerator magnets in a variety of whimsical shapes and designs. You'd need the magnetic material from about seven dead human bodies to make a one-ounce magnet, let alone a magnet powerful enough to chase down a wily roadrunner.

Wired

Use #60: Copper Goods

Copper utensils were first used by primitive men about 8,000 years ago. The ease at which copper could be mined and fashioned into tools made it the first widely used metal, allowing early Egyptian, Asian and European craftsmen to construct sturdy buildings, works of art, and weapons of war.

Modern men do urban battle with copper every

time they employ the copper wiring in their PDA's, motor down the highway in cars powered by copper-infused motors, and watch their favorite sports team on a television containing copper parts. Copper has adapted to modern times thanks to its high conductivity, as most of the copper mined around the world is used to make copper wiring for the electronics industry.

72 milligrams of copper can be found in the human body. According to www.copper.org, the scant amount of copper in the human body prevents anemia and bone disease, battles cell damage and assists in fetal and infant development. It also promotes energy production, which is appropriate considering its industrial uses.

The puny amount of copper in one dead human body could fit on the head of a pin, necessitating a lot of copper donors to produce anything of value. For example:

--a typical car contains about 50 pounds of copper, requiring the copper contributions of about 314,995 dead human bodies (the population of Detroit, MI, could provide the copper content for about three cars)

--a Boeing 474-200 contains about 180 pounds of copper, demanding the copper content of about 1.13 million dead human bodies (the population of Boeing-headquartered Chicago, IL could provide the copper content for about two and a half jet planes)

--a Triton-class nuclear submarine uses about 100 tons of copper, equivalent to the copper content of about 1.26

billion dead human bodies (the world's population could provide the copper content for about five nuclear submarines).

If a nuclear submarine sounds like overkill, then a mere 2,778 dead human bodies could provide enough copper to make a small mace head (circa 3000-2000 BC), thus allowing you to get in touch with your primitive side while texting your fantasy football buddies.

Chapter 16
Communication

"Rosabelle-answer-tell-pray, answer-look-tell-answer, answer-tell."

Harry Houdini
Famous magician and escape artist

Houdini was a life-long skeptic who made great sport of exposing charlatans who claimed they could speak to the dead. But he was also hopeful that communication with the dead was possible, so he and his wife, Rosabelle, created a secret phrase that Houdini would say to her after his death.

Houdini would've been better served using materials from a dead human body for earthly communication, as the following chapter illustrates.

The Write Stuff
Use #61: Pencil "Lead"

Despite the name, there's no actual lead in a pencil. What is commonly known as pencil "lead" is actually a combination of graphite and clay. Pencils with a high graphite content make soft, thick marks; the addition of clay makes the graphite harder. The amount of "lead" in a pencil depends on its consistency and where it was made, though one gram of graphite and clay in most pencils is a fair estimate.

Graphite is a form of carbon, the building block of all life and the second most common element in the human body. If the 16 kilograms (35.3 pounds) of carbon in one dead human body were distilled as black, flaky graphite, it could manufacture enough "lead" for 16,000 pencils. The pencil script would be soft without the addition of clay, making it useful in sketching, children's pencils…and composing poison-pen letters with your people-procured pencil "lead."

Pencil Facts

If you ever meet noted academic and prolific author Henry Petroski, ask him if he wrote his 1990 book, The Pencil: A History of Design and Circumstance, *with an actual pencil.*

Early Romans and Greeks pioneered an early type of pencil by making notations on papyrus with lead cakes.

Artists during the Middle Ages used metal styluses to make impressions on writing surfaces.

Graphite sheathed in a wooden case (the precursor to the modern pencil) was first used during the 1500's.

Carbon Copy
Use #62: Copier Ink

Frustrated by mounting paperwork and the onset of arthritis, patent clerk Chester Carlson set out to invent a quick and easy way to make document reproductions. After several years of study, Carlson and his collaborator, physicist Otto Kornei, created the first xerograph in 1938, later popularized as a Xerox copy. Millions of naked butt prints at drunken office parties would soon follow.

Cheekiness aside, Carlson's invention revolutionized the printed word. The process works by means of static electricity: an electrically charged cylinder inside the copy machine interacts with the light and dark images on the original page. The dark images on the page (like the typeface you're reading right now) leave a positive electrostatic impression on the cylinder.

Negatively charged toner is then dusted over the cylinder. Opposites attract, so the negatively charged toner sticks to the areas of the cylinder containing a positive charge, which creates a pattern identical to the original page. The toner is then spit onto a blank piece of paper, warmed, and pressed as it exits the machine.

Modern printers use toner made of several ingredients, including polymers, pigments, and carbon black. Though carbon black is sometimes contaminated with toxic chemicals, in its basic state carbon black is simply carbon, like the 16 kilograms that can be found in one dead human body.

Between 1%-5% of the total ingredients in a bottle of toner is carbon black. Assuming an amount of 5%, one dead human body could provide the carbon content for about 1,454 cartridges (220 grams of toner in each). If each cartridge can produce 6000 pages, that's over 8.7 million total pages.

Pure carbon was used to print documents in Chester Carlson's day. If we equipped modern cartridges with pure carbon and assumed the same results, the carbon from one dead human body could fill about 72 cartridges, yielding 432,000 pages.

Copier Facts

The toxic chemicals sometimes found in toner make it a carcinogen, a cancer-causing substance.

Cash In Your Chips
Use #63: Computer Chips

Thousands of years of scientific experiments are responsible for the technical advancements described in this book. The combined knowledge of these efforts is enormous, but it could all be stored on one tiny computer chip made of silicon.

Silicon is the second most abundant element in the earth's crust, but the silicon used in computers is rare due to the intense engineering involved to create pure, wafer-thin chips. Silica is mined, cooked and heated with other elements to create silicon that is 98% pure, then further purified, formed into rods, and finally sliced into thin strips about the size of a fingernail.

If that sounds too labor-intensive, you could dig deep within yourself and extract the one gram of silicon found in your own body. Better yet, dig deep within nine dead human bodies, because many computers contain nine grams of silicon. Combine that with batteries and copper wires, and you've got the makings for a state-of-the-art machine…and a human body.

Computer Chip Facts

The "clean rooms" in which silicon is refined are cleaner than hospital operating rooms, and those that manufacture it dress like surgeons to insure an exceptional level of purity.

Chapter 17
Home and Garden

Ever heard the urban legend about Lupe Velez? She was a Hollywood starlet during the 1930's who appeared in dozens of films. By the age of 36 her star had dimmed and an out-of-wedlock pregnancy threatened her reputation, so she decided to take her own life in a way that she hoped would always be remembered: dressed in a silver lamé gown, Lupe swallowed several sleeping pills and retired to her bed.

Unfortunately, she indulged in her favorite Mexican meal first, which didn't sit well with the sleeping pills. As detailed in Kenneth Anger's book *Hollywood Babylon*, Lupe rushed to the toilet, slipped, and fell headfirst into the bowl. She was discovered in that position with a broken neck. It wasn't what she intended, but she's been remembered ever since.

Death is a dirty business. So is housework, so it's convenient that many common cleaning products, plant and pest supplies, and other household goods could be fashioned from the remains of a tidy human corpse.

I Took Myself to the Cleaners
Use #64: Laundry Detergent

In 1909 Maytag produced the first engine-powered washing machine, the *Hired Girl Washer*. Little did they know their benign cleaning tool would someday become an instrument of death.

Or so claimed the email that began circulating in the late 1990's about Samuel Randolph Strickson, who allegedly died in a freak laundry accident. The email, which exists in many variations, contends that Strickson tried to overfill his machine by pushing the clothing down with his feet. He accidentally hit the *on* switch, and a series of slapstick events ensued in which he spun around violently, slammed against a wall, and was finally killed by a blow to his head. Oh, and his dog peed on a spilled box of baking soda, causing it to explode.

That's an unlikely series of events, though over the years washing machines have caused a number of freak accidents. Tragic stories abound of young children playing where they shouldn't and either suffocating or dying after being thrashed about in an active machine. Another news story involved a laundry company employee who died from hyperthermia (overheating) after becoming trapped in an industrial-size washing machine while trying to clear a blockage.

Manufacturers have gone to great lengths in recent years to prevent future washing machine mishaps. Modern machines are equipped with mechanisms that prevent the washing cycle from beginning if the lid is still open. Some machines remain locked shut for several seconds after the machine has stopped. These safety precautions will hopefully spare the likes of Samuel Randolph Strickland, fictional or not, from ever falling foul of a soapy fate.

But if you still insist on being an active participant in the laundry process, consider something less graphic: the human body contains 18 milligrams of boron, an ingredient in the popular laundry detergent additive Borax. Now go clean yourself.

Life's In Bloom
Use #65: Plant Food & Weed Killer

It's easy to kill a plant, as many budding horticulturalists know. Unfortunately, killing the weeds that plague plant life is not so easy. Take heart in knowing that one dead human body contains the elements that can help a plant blossom and wipe out pesky weeds.

As we learned in the previous use, boron is a key ingredient in laundry detergent, but it's also important in plant growth. Boron is essential to many plant functions, including pollination, seed reproduction, and normal cell division. Boron fertilizer bolsters crops that suffer from boron deficiency.

After you've saved your crops, rescue your lawn from the scourge of weeds by using the seven milligrams of arsenic in the human body.

Herbicide is a chemical solution used to destroy plants, especially weeds. Though highly toxic and under frequent safety evaluation, arsenic and its many compounds are used in popular herbicides like All-In-One Weed Killer.

Your level of devotion to your plants is entirely up to you, but any true horticulturalist would die in defense of his crops…and if you believe that, you won't mind making a similar sacrifice for the next use.

Little Buggers
Use #66: Insect Killer

If you were willing to mine a dead human body for fertilizer and herbicide, you'll love contributing to the extermination of bugs and other varmints.

Just as boron gives life to ailing plants, it can also rid your home and garden of insects. Boric acid, a compound of boron, is a mild acid used in insecticide. Combined with hydrogen and oxygen, one dead human body could produce 46.33 milligrams of boric acid. Likewise, arsenic also serves as a potent ingredient in certain types of insecticides.

For bigger pests, the 0.5 milligrams of thallium in one dead human body is an element once used in rat poison. Thallium is a soft, silvery-white metal that can be absorbed through the skin. It is highly toxic and rarely used, which has led to its strict regulation or outright prohibition in many countries.

But don't let that deter you from eliminating any and all pests that might intrude on your outdoor pursuits. Just monitor your thallium use carefully, otherwise the bugs and rats might be rid of you.

Foiled Again
Use #67: Aluminum Foil

Aluminum foil can do more than keep food fresh. The official Reynolds Wrap website (www.reynoldskitchens.com) offers a bevy of creative uses, including grilling tips, baking instructions and arts and crafts projects.

Better yet, consider staging an aluminum foil art exhibit. Avant-garde sculptor Tom Friedman, known for his artistic creations using common household items like tooth picks and toilet paper, staged an exhibit in 2007 at the Lever House Lobby Gallery consisting of artwork crafted entirely out of aluminum foil. The centerpiece sculpture, *Aluminum Foil Thing*, included aluminum foil animals, letters and numbers, giant nuts and bolts, and silver spirals.

If all else fails, you can use aluminum foil to construct a hat. Any space cadet will tell you that wearing an aluminum foil hat allows you to communicate with aliens, block telepathic commands, and prevent the government from reading your mind. (Actually, the exact specifications of an aluminum foil hat depend on the person wearing it.)

Why so many uses? Because if you're going to plunder one dead human body for its 60 milligrams of aluminum, you'd better have a darn good reason.

Odds and Ends

Use #68: Various Household Products

A bevy of common household appliances could be constructed using elements found in the human body.

The 20 micrograms of tungsten in one dead human body could be useful in light bulbs. Tungsten is a metal that maintains its hardness under extreme temperatures and has a high melting point, making it ideal for light bulb filaments.

Yttrium is an oft overlooked element, not as well-known or easy to pronounce as most metals, but the 0.6 milligrams of yttrium in one dead human body has a variety of uses, like generating red color in a television screen. Lucille Ball's hair and Dorothy's ruby slippers wouldn't be the same without it.

Germanium is a silvery-white metalloid that has many industrial uses, like manufacturing special types of glass. The five milligrams of germanium in one dead human body could be used to make wide angle camera lenses and fluorescent lamps.

And finally, tantalum is a shiny, silvery metal useful in electronics. In powder form, tantalum makes the capacitors used in portable phones, pagers and personal computers. In fact, the ever-shrinking size of portable phones is largely thanks to tantalum. Your body contains 0.2 milligrams. A little goes a long way.

Chapter 18
Fashionably Dead

A platinum cast-replica of a real 18th century human skull made by British artist Damien Hirst was bought by an unnamed investment firm in 2007 for 100 million dollars. Titled "For the Love of God," it was encrusted with 8,601 diamonds, totaling 1,106.18 carats--accentuated by a large diamond in the middle of the forehead that alone cost 4.2 million dollars.

If that's out of your price range, there are other ways a dead human body can make a fashion statement. Egyptian mummies were once plundered for ingredients to make art supplies, and dead human bodies could also be used to fashion clothing, furniture, and fine jewelry.

I'd Give You the Skin Off My Back...Want It?
Use #69: Leather Goods

With the cost of quality leather goods skyrocketing, you may want to consider an alternate source of fabric.

The average human body is covered with about two square yards of skin, a valuable commodity in the garment industry. That much skin could produce 52 small purses, or 12 large handbags.

The skin (or pelt, if you will) from one dead human body could produce two leather jackets, or a couple of leather aprons. That much material could also produce about 72 belts, depending on waist size, or you could maximize your human pelt by making a man-size rug.

Aunt Bessie Lets People Walk All Over Her

Before human skin can be used to make luxury handbags, rugs and other textiles, it has to be prepared using strict tanning procedures. If we assume that human skin is similar to cowhide, the process will require a fair amount of time and grunt work.

First, you'll need a sturdy skinning knife with a curved edge, made of heavy steel and well-sharpened. Cowhide is easiest to remove when the carcass is still warm, so you might want to camp-out beside your dear Aunt Bessie's death bed so you can jump into action once she expires.

Small and medium sized animals can be hoisted up a tree, making the skinning process easier. If your Aunt Bessie was a petite lady, or if you can find a sturdy branch capable of supporting her weight, hang that old girl upside down and slice open her throat to drain her bodily fluids. Don't worry about the mess--Aunt Bessie won't mind.

Before skinning Aunt Bessie it's a good idea to remove her head, arms and legs. These are difficult areas to skin and are best discarded at the start. (If the thought of beheading your dear Auntie seems distasteful, consider how distasteful it would be to see Aunt Bessie's face staring at you from the top of a throw rug or the collar of a leather jacket. Not so good, huh?) Make your first incision beginning under the chin and move down the stomach in an even line before finishing at the tail (that would be Aunt Bessie's derriere).

Next, loosen the skin from her abdomen by using sweeping knife strokes, but be careful not to puncture Aunt Bessie's skin while you work the knife underneath her hide. Once a sufficient amount of skin has been loosened from her stomach, use your fingers to peel off the skin along her back and rump.

By now you should have a good view of your former Aunt Bessie, inside and out. Finish the skinning process by hanging Aunt Bessie's skin out to dry or lay it on a concrete floor for six to eight hours. Cure her skin with salt if you don't finish preparing it immediately, otherwise you can continue the tanning process once her body heat has dissipated.

Stretch her skin across wooden planks and use a dull knife or large bone--ah, another use for Aunt Bessie's body!-- to scrape off any remaining fatty tissue from the underside of her skin, then soak her skin in cold water for several days. If Aunt Bessie was a furry lady, use hardwood ashes, lime or lye to remove her body hair before soaking her skin in a final tanning solution. If you plan to use her pelt as a rug, feel free to leave her hair just as you found it. Just don't tell the neighbors where you found your new rug.

Color Me Dead
Use #70: Clothing Dye

The final step in the tanning process involves soaking your human pelt in a tanning solution. There are many types of tanning solutions, including a mixture of cool water and chromium salt.

Chromium salt is composed of chromium, oxygen, hydrogen and sodium, all of which can be found in one dead human body. The tiny amount of chromium in the human body will require a significant body count to produce enough for our purposes, so cross your fingers and hope that more of your relatives follow dear Aunt Bessie into the great beyond. And keep their pelts, too, so you can fashion a matching collection.

And consider adding color to your human pelts

by using other ingredients found in the human body. The bromine in one dead human body is a common ingredient in many fabric dyes, along with selenium, which is used to create red dye, and nickel, which is used to create green dye.

A dye's effectiveness depends on the thickness of the pelt, so expect some difficulty if your Aunt Bessie was known for her thick skin. Contacting a professional leather dealer is a smart move, though expect some blowback when you reveal the source of your pelt. Some people are touchy that way.

A Hairy Situation
Use #71: Human Hair Wigs

Companies that produce hair replacement products for commercial and charitable organizations sometimes use real human hair. It's natural appearance makes it ideal for those who suffer from hair loss due to an illness, while hair extensions and toupees are popular with anyone whose own scalp leaves something to be desired.

Locks of Love (www.locksoflove.org) is an organization that provides children who suffer from medical hair loss with quality hair prosthetics. The custom-made hairpieces, which normally retail for $3,500 to $6,000, donated by Locks of Love are instrumental in returning a positive self-image to children afflicted by a disease.

For more ambitious fro-merchants, buyandsellhair.com bills itself as the #1 global human hair marketplace on the internet. The website allows users to list their locks for auction to the highest bidder, complete with hair biographies, detailed dimensions and pictures. All types of hair are welcome, though chemically unblemished hair free of harsh treatments (such as curling irons, sun damage, perms--often referred to as "virgin hair") is preferred.

Long, healthy hair fetches the highest bids. Men may feel deterred from participating, but consider this: the length of a man's beard if he never shaves would exceed thirty feet by the end of his life. The current record bid on Buy and Sell Hair is $2,500 for 27 inches of virgin brown hair. Maybe men should throw away their razors and invest in mustache combs instead.

Viva la Revolution

Hair clipped from the head of Socialist revolutionary Ernesto "Che" Guevara sold at auction in 2007 for $100,000. The controversial tresses, which were collected by the CIA shortly after Guevara was killed by the Bolivian military, were purchased by a Texas bookstore owner who collects 1960's memorabilia. The three-inch lock of hair will undoubtedly pop up on t-shirts and dorm room posters for many years to come.

Paint It, Brown
Use #72: Brown Paint Dye

Unlucky in love and suffering from mental illness, Vincent Van Gogh had the bright idea to cut off his ear and present it to the object of his affection, a prostitute. Hard to believe the severed appendage didn't win her over, though afterward Van Gogh painted his classic *Self-Portrait with Bandage (*1889), depicting his head wrapped in surgical dressing.

At least Van Gogh's efforts weren't completely in vain, an important lesson for every artist about the merits of artistic redemption. Still, if you don't want to saw off your ear for the sake of a classic painting, consider other ways a human body could be used to compose a work of art.

Egyptian mummies have suffered many harsh treatments over the years, some of which are depicted in this book, including this recipe for brown paint that includes mashed-up mummy remains: after grinding a mummy down to a fine powder, the remaining pigment residue can be used as a painter's dye. First concocted in the 16th or 17th centuries, the distinctive deep brown hue created by the mummy powder was referred to as mummy brown and Egyptian brown.

Egyptian mummy powder in watercolor and oil paintings continued for hundreds of years until popular knowledge of the controversial practice halted its production. Modern paint makers approximate the look of mummy brown by using naturally occurring minerals instead of thousand year-old dead bodies, which may calm the watchdogs of good taste but doesn't paint nearly as indelible a picture.

If you'd still like to mine a dead person for art supplies, consider using the many individual elements found in the human body. The tiny amount of bismuth in one dead human body can serve as an additive in oil paint, while the fair amount of chlorine can also serve as a principle ingredient. For a splash of color, the aluminum in one dead human body is a key component in silver paint, while chromium is used in yellow paint, manganese for brown paint, and molybdenum for red, yellow and orange paint.

You're a Real Gem
Use #73: Cubic Zirconia Jewelry

A 2003 article in the *China Daily* newspaper reported a would-be jewel thief's attempt to steal a diamond ring. Surveillance cameras caught the woman as she swallowed the $20,000 trinket while shopping in a Florida jewelry store. She denied perpetrating the theft until an x-ray confirmed the location of the pricey bauble, so authorities kept her in detention until nature took its course and she deposited the diamond ring into the hands of waiting police investigators.

There are better, legal, and cleaner ways to produce shiny eye candy from a human body. Put vanity aside and consider cubic zirconia, a cheap and realistic substitute for real diamonds.

Cubic zirconia is the crystalline form of zirconium dioxide, made with zirconium and oxygen. Both elements can be found in one dead human body and together could produce one milligram of zirconium dioxide. Cubic zirconia appears realistic to the casual eye, is easily shaped and can be colored to the buyer's specification. Just don't attend any eyeglass conventions as cubic zirconia is detectable under close scrutiny.

Lab-created alexandrite jewelry can also be crafted from the contents of a dead person. The .11 mg of vanadium in one dead human body is an important ingredient in synthetic alexandrite gemstones, along with aluminum oxide, which can also be formed with the aluminum and oxygen in one dead human body.

Real gemstones are formed over many years under intense pressure and heat deep inside the Earth's crust. Synthetic gemstones are a shortcut to natural beauty…but if you consider the condition your body will be in during its excavation, the process will hardly seem like a cheat.

Hell's Furnishings
Use #74: Human Skin Lampshades

One of the horror stories of World War II is that the Nazis used skin from executed Holocaust prisoners to manufacture lampshades.

The story first emerged near the end of the war with the release several Holocaust-themed documentaries including *Death Mills* (1945), a short film made by famed director Billy Wilder and available to view at the U.S. Holocaust Memorial Museum website (http://www.ushmm.org/). The stark 22-minute film, shot on location at several newly liberated concentration camps, depicts emaciated survivors clinging to life and the inhuman living conditions to which they were subjected. The film also describes how charred human remains were sold to farmers as fertilizer, how human hair was clipped from corpses and sold to manufacturers, and how gold teeth were pulled from the mouths of lifeless victims. As the narrator intoned, "The Nazi butchers wasted as little of the body as possible."

Not shown on the website's copy of the film is a scene shot in the living quarters of Buchenwald Concentration Camp commandant Karl Koch and his wife, Isle. A long-rumored but hard-to-find still photo attributed to the film supposedly depicts a collection of atrocities, including shrunken heads, tattooed human skin, and a common-looking lamp which the narrator described as "a lampshade made of human skin."

A separate documentary available on the U.S.H.M.M. website, *German Civilians Visit Buchenwald*, depicts German citizens walking past a display table containing Nazi atrocities. The caption reads, "German civilians on the grounds viewing a table display of paintings on human skins, lampshade made of human skin, various parts of the human body preserved in alcohol and two heads which were shrunk to one-fifth their normal size."

It's hard to discount even the most brutal reports of Nazi atrocities in light of the indisputable supporting evidence, but using human skin for lampshades has inspired a fair amount of skepticism. Whether an urban legend or not, human skin lampshades do attest to the Nazi's unimaginable horrors.

On a Brighter Note…

The human body contains three important elements used to make halogen light bulbs. Light from a halogen light bulb is created when a tungsten filament sealed inside a transparent tube reacts with a halogen element like iodine or bromine. One human body contains tungsten, iodine, and bromine, so by all means, let your inner light shine through.

Chapter 19
Corpses on Parade

Vincent Price played a disfigured sculptor in 1953's *House of Wax* who creates exquisite models that are actually real human bodies covered in wax; his latest exhibit coincides with the disappearance of several corpses from the local morgue. His depraved plans escalate when he meets a beautiful young woman who would make a perfect Marie Antoinette, the centerpiece in his house of human horrors.

Vincent Price flicks aren't known for their subtlety or realism, but the movie's theme is nothing new. Human corpses have been displayed throughout history as a way to impose order and fear among a dissenting public, celebrate and maintain social norms, and honor legendary celebrities.

Recent human body displays showcase the artistic and educational qualities of a well-preserved stiff, and look surprisingly similar to Price's creations. For those who wish to create their own PDA's (public displays of affliction) there are methods of animal preservation that could also be applied to the human body.

JIM
MORRISON
RIP

Don't Make Me Get Cross With You
Use #75: Crucifixion

Crucifixion was a method of capital punishment...whereby the outstretched arms of the victim were tied or nailed to a crossbeam, which was then laid in a groove across the top or suspended by means of a notch in the side of an upright stake...because of its cruelty, crucifixion was intended as both a severe punishment of the victim and a frightful deterrent to others.

--New Catholic Encyclopedia

Imagine hanging from a cross, suspended by twin spikes driven through your wrists, gasping for breath as your chest muscles tighten under intense pressure. If you don't suffocate, you might bleed to death from the bloody lashing you suffered earlier in the day. If not that, sun exposure will dehydrate you after several days, or the weary executioner will tire of waiting and finally plunge a spear into your heart--provided your heart hasn't already exploded. However you die, the defining characteristic of your crucifixion is public shame. You will be on display during the last agonizing moments of your life, and then for some time after.

A sign called a titulus will be attached to the top of your cross describing your crime so that passersby will be deterred from committing the same offense. You will be crucified near the location of your crime, or in a heavily trafficked area where you will be commonly seen. As the Roman rhetorician Quintilian wrote, "whenever we crucify the guilty, the most crowded roads are chosen, where most people can see and be moved by this fear. For penalties relate not so much to retribution as to their exemplary effect."

Quintilian's cold appraisal proved true following the slave rebellion of the Third Servile War (or Gladiator War, famously depicted in the 1960 Kirk Douglas starrer *Spartacus*). The Roman army crushed the 120,000-strong slave revolt after two years of conflict, then discouraged future uprisings by crucifying 6,000 rebel slaves along the two kilometer road between Rome and Capua.

Crucifixion was banned in the Roman Empire in 337 AD by the first Christian emperor Constantine the Great out of respect to Christ, but the practice continued around the world for many years. Japanese crucifixion involved needling the victim's body with thin spears for several hours; if the executioner was paid a sufficient bribe, he would pierce the heart early in the process. Either way, the body was left to hang for some time after death. Crucifixion was last used in France in 1127 to execute Bertholde, who assassinated Charles the Righteous. It remains a form of discipline under modern Islamic code.

If That Doesn't Quite Nail It…

If crucifixion is a bit too biblical for your taste, here are a few other intimidating methods of public execution.

"I have therefore determined that after your

execution you shall be hung in chains until the fowls of the air pick the flesh of your body and your bones bleach and whiten in the winds of heaven," pronounced the Lord Justice Clerk of Scotland when sentencing Alexander Gillam to death in 1810, "thereby to afford a constant warning of the fatal consequences which almost invariably attend the indulgence of the passions." Whatever "passions" Gillam indulged in, they were bad enough that others needed to be discouraged from doing the same.

In a bid to fight the rising crime rate in Britain, the Murder Act of 1752 ordered that convicted felons be hung within 48 hours of conviction and their bodies be dissected or gibbeted. Gibbeting involved publicly displaying an executed criminal by rope, cage, or some other means of suspension, which isn't nearly as cute as the name "gibbet" implies. Neither was the final act of a guillotine execution, in which the victim's severed head was hoisted atop a poll for everyone to see. The message: crime is nothing to lose your head over.

Crucifixion Fact

Crucifixion was first used by the Phoenicians about 1000 years before the birth of Christ.

Better than a Lucky Rabbit's Foot

After viewing a public execution (the guillotine and hanging were particular crowd pleasers), the executioner would sometimes slice off the victim's hands, feet, and other extremities and give them to the witnesses. Body parts from an executed criminal were thought to bring good fortune, despite the bad fortune experienced by the previous owner.

Communist Corpse
Use #76: Soviet Propaganda

"Lenin lived, Lenin lives, Lenin will live."
--Russian Poet Vladimir Mayakovski

Mayakovski expressed the feelings of many Russians after the death of Communist leader Vladimir Lenin in 1924, but his slogan also embodied the attitude of the Politburo, the Russian political bureau, when they decided to display Lenin's body in one of the weirdest political statements of the 20th century.

The Politburo ordered Lenin's body removed from his home shortly after his death and made arrangements to display him beside the Kremlin Wall in Red Square, located in the heart of Moscow. A special wooden structure was constructed to accommodate the 100,000 mourners who viewed the body during the first six weeks alone. Preservationists soon determined that his remains could be preserved for much longer than initially thought.

A lot longer, as a matter of fact. One account describes the liquid used to preserve Lenin as a mixture of glycerin and potassium acetate called balsam, which is injected into Lenin's corpse regularly. The sarcophagus, which was upgraded to a stone mausoleum in 1930, is kept at a brisk 62 degrees and 80-90% humidity. A tailor periodically replaces his clothing, which fades over time, while artisans use a variety of tools, including hydrogen peroxide, to restore a healthy visage to Lenin's face. Despite these efforts, his corpse has become waxy-looking over time, though that didn't stop the estimated 10 million people who visited Lenin's mausoleum during its first 50 years.

The goodwill of millions of Soviets rested in Lenin's cold, dead hands. Communist leaders, especially Lenin's successor, Joseph Stalin, wished to use that goodwill to mask harsh "reforms" that oppressed millions of people. In his book, *Lenin: A Biography*, Robert Service says the Politburo and Stalin, "believed that the corpse in the mausoleum would serve as an object of unifying importance for the citizens of the USSR and for the followers of Communism around the world." The Politburo used Lenin's body to keep his spirit alive and hide their activities behind the nationalism that Lenin inspired.

After the fall of Communism in the early 1990's, many suggested that Lenin's remains should be removed from the mausoleum and properly buried. But by then public sentiment had grown for the unfortunate stiff, who has since become a lucrative tourist attraction. Communism may be history, but a small part of it lives on in the body of a dead man.

Lenin Facts

The thought of using Lenin's corpse as a political tool struck many as distasteful, including his wife, Nadezhda Konstantinovna, which she stated in a letter that was classified for many years: "When the project arose among our people to bury V.I. in the Kremlin, I was filled with terrible indignation."

Anyone who wishes to view Lenin's body may do so between the hours of 10:00 AM-1:00 PM any day except Monday and Friday. Photographs and home videos are not allowed, and visitors should expect a long line for the popular exhibit.

Rockin' the Afterlife
Use #77: Celebrity Gravesites

Jim Morrison jumped the gun when he wrote "The End," his 12-minute hallucinogenic dirge about death. As his own gravesite demonstrates, death can lead to a whole new beginning as a rock-and-roll landmark.

Morrison was found dead in his Paris apartment at the age of 27, bloated due to a bad diet and heavy drug and alcohol abuse. His body was buried in a nondescript grave in Pe're-Lachaise Cemetery, which proved insufficient in 1986 when two grave robbers tried to dig up his body. An elaborate headstone and bust of Morrison were soon added, though the bust has since been stolen and the headstone and surrounding structures have been marked with graffiti.

Thousands make the trek to Pe're-Lachaise every year to camp out by the gravesite, sing songs, read

Morrison's poetry, and smoke weed. A graveyard is an unusual place to find a gift shop, though anyone looking for souvenirs will likely find joints, pills, and plastic lighters left behind by well-wishers. Of course, if you wish to avoid Morrison's fate, you should probably skip the souvenirs.

Elvis Lived Here...and Still Does

Elvis Presley was also overweight and in the thralls of drug addiction when he died at the age of 42 in 1977. His Memphis, Tennessee home, Graceland, was converted into a museum complete with a guided tour that includes Elvis's gravesite. His tombstone has fueled many conspiracy theories as the spelling of his middle name, "Aaron,' contains one additional "a" than the spelling he used during his lifetime, suggesting to some that the grave is fake and Elvis is still alive.

Graceland is the second most visited home in America, second only to the White House. A cottage industry has sprung up around the residence, with nearby hotel accommodations catering to Presley fans and a local music scene inspired by his legacy. The week of his death (August 17th) inspires the largest commemorative celebrations of the year, proof that remembering a man's death can be a fitting tribute to his life.

Dead Celebrity Facts

Margaret Burk and Gary Hudson's Final Curtain: Eternal Resting Places of Hundreds of Stars, Celebrities, Moguls, Misers and Misfits, *offers readers a detailed listing of dozens of celebrity cemeteries. The book hasn't been updated in a number of years, not that the subjects of the book are going anywhere.*

Weird Science
Use #78: Plastination

Plastination makes it possible to preserve individual tissues and organs that have been removed from the body of the deceased as well as the entire body itself.

--Body Worlds website

Plastination inventor Gunther von Hagens cuts a striking figure in his dapper, black fedora hat, but he's not half as striking as the anatomical models he creates using real human bodies.

Von Hagens' controversial process involves draining every drop of fluid from a human corpse to be replaced with a liquid polymer (plastic) that preserves the body, which is then displayed as anatomical artwork. If that sounds hunky-dory to you, than you're in luck, because von Hagens eagerly accepts volunteers.

Von Hagens invented Plastination in 1975 while working at the Institute of Pathology and Anatomy at Heidelberg University. His creations, which resemble waxy replicas of human beings, are sliced open to reveal the human body in ways that have never been seen before.

In addition to whole bodies, display tables showcase individual body parts. One display shows a healthy, pink lung beside a slightly darker smokers lung next to a charbroiled coal miners lung. Other tables show human hearts in different stages of disease, amputated limbs and discombobulated eyeballs.

One controversial, but admittedly compelling, display shows a pregnant woman who died shortly before childbirth. Part of her stomach is cut away to show the preserved, unborn fetus still inside. Additional jars contain unborn fetuses plastinated at different stages of development.

Other controversies persist, including the accusation that Von Hagens acquired dead bodies from hospitals in Kyrgyzstan and prisons in China for use in his experiments. The nature of his work has also led many countries to ban his exhibitions and pursue prosecution against him for disturbing the dead. To counter charges that he uses unwilling participants, sign-up tables are erected at all Body Worlds exhibitions.

Some examples from the Body Worlds Exhibition

--A skateboarder, without skin, posed while balancing on one hand to show extreme muscle contraction during intense physical activity

--A skeleton stripped of everything except its plastinated veins to show the scope of the circulatory system

--Two athletes stripped to their musculature, one a baseball player positioned like a player at bat, the other

a javelin thrower with its body arched in mid-throw

--A single body dissected into hundreds of pieces, each piece hung from the ceiling by invisible wire and positioned as if the pieces are being pulled away from the center of the body. In this fashion every layer of the human anatomy, from the outer surface to the inner core, can be seen, resembling an exploding marionette.

Fit to be Stuffed
Use #79: Human Body Taxidermy

In October 2004, the *Phoenix New Times* ran a cover story about *Preserve a Life*, an organization that offers to taxidermy your recently deceased loved one. The article explained at length how a dead relative's skin is "pickled," or "freeze dried," then stretched over a lightweight fiberglass mannequin. Among the many clients profiled were a family that had their grandmother "humidermied" so that she could remain a part of their household; a dead little boy who was mounted on a scooter and dressed in his favorite shirt; and others who only had their heads mounted or limbs preserved, such as the wife who preserved her husband's hand for use as an ashtray holder.

If that short synopsis caused one or both of your eyebrows to raise, than your sharper than many readers who didn't realize the newspaper was playing a Halloween prank. To support the gag, the paper included doctored photographs to compliment their story, created a believable corporate history for *Preserve a Life*, and even constructed a modest website to support the fictional business. The article's writer, Stephen Lemons, even managed to fool members of the national media, including producers from the television newsmagazines *Primetime Live* and *20/20*.

While some weirdos may think that human taxidermy is a fitting way to honor a dead acquaintance, local laws prohibiting human body desecration prevent the practice from being performed. But good taste and local statutes are hardly impediments to a fertile imagination.

If you'd like to be stuffed and mounted after you die, here's what you'll need to do:

--Arrange to have your skin removed and cured in accordance with proper tanning procedures (see Use #69). A properly mounted animal will retain only its outer hide, so be prepared to lose your internal organs and anything else that cannot be saved (your eyeballs and teeth will be replaced with glass decoys once your skin is mounted; you may want to consider donating your organs in accordance with Use #25)

--Ask a talented sculptor to create a cast replica of your body using fiberglass, wire, or any other suitable material that is durable but also lightweight...hey, just because your dead doesn't mean you should be cumbersome, right?

--Hire a trained taxidermist to mount your chemically treated skin. It's important to hire someone who knows what he's doing so your skin doesn't tear or stretch during the mounting process. You may want to specify ahead of time if you'd like your body posed in a particular manner, whether your eyes should be open or closed, and what you would like to wear post-taxidermy.

For added value, you could employ your dead body to perform a useful task, like serving as a hat rack or a clothing store mannequin. Just don't model a fur coat, otherwise you'll be protested by both human and animal rights activists.

Chapter 20
Travel and Recreation

Charcoal is created by burning a carbon-rich substance, like wood, sawdust or limestone, in a low-oxygen environment. Henry Ford's auto plants produced a lot of sawdust and scrap wood, inspiring the automobile pioneer to mass produce wood-fueled briquettes (under the brand-name *Kingsford*) and market the product to new car owners looking for a weekend activity.

And so began two great American pastimes: the family picnic and gratuitous fossil fuel consumption. Travel and recreation have gone hand and hand ever since, so it's appropriate that dead human bodies could be used to do both.

Corpse on Wheels
Use #80: Crash Test Dummies

If you want to get the most bang for your dead body buck, use a dead human body in an automobile crash test. As reported by the New York Times in 1993, that's exactly what researchers at Wayne State University did in a program financed by the federal government, General Motors and the Ford Motor Company. According to the university's Bio-Engineering Center, between 30-40 human corpses were used in a three-year period to test how a car crash impacts the human body.

Similar experiments conducted by Germany's Heidelberg University supposedly used over 200 corpses during a 20-year period. The Vatican condemned Heidelberg when the university's testing was finally disclosed, though administrators at Wayne State reported no objections to their program since all of their test subjects were approved by family members.

Dr. Albert King, who oversaw the Wayne State program, defended the practice as an invaluable tool to saving human lives--another example of how the dead can offer the living a helping hand.

Dead on Arrival

Before the invention of the automobile, bicycling was a practical and recreational form of transportation enjoyed by millions of people around the world. Bicycles are still popular today in developing countries and urban areas choked by pollution and traffic congestion.

Titanium is a strong, lightweight, corrosion-resistant metal used to construct bicycle frames and other components; one dead human body contains 20 milligrams. The human body also possesses 4.2 grams of iron, which is used to construct bicycles and automobiles. Collect enough dead bodies and you could build your own car, outfitted with steel-belted radial tires made with cobalt--one dead human body contains three milligrams of cobalt.

Our Flight Was a Real Blast
Use #81: Hindenburg Hydrogen

The Hindenburg was a gas-filled dirigible, three times longer than today's commercial aircraft. It was built by Nazi Germany and outfitted with luxurious amenities and a spectacular view of the earth below. The Hindenburg was supposed to be inflated with non-flammable helium gas, produced exclusively in the United States at the time. But the U.S. government restricted the sale of helium to the Germans, fearing the Nazi regime would use the gas for military purposes.

Instead, German engineers modified the vessel with flame resistant materials and filled it with hydrogen, a highly flammable gas. Despite their precautions, the large amount of hydrogen contained in the Hindenburg was ignited by a spark on its 21st voyage, possibly caused by static electricity or a lightning bolt, as it prepared to land in Lakehurst, New Jersey three days after it departed Frankfurt, Germany. 36 passengers, crew members and a spectator died during the crash. The entire aircraft was engulfed in flames a mere 34 seconds after the first fire erupted.

If you'd like to throw caution to the wind, you can plump up your own dirigible with the seven kilograms of hydrogen found in one dead human body. If the fate of the Hindenburg has taught you a valuable lesson, you can opt to fill it with the miniscule amount of helium also found in the human body. Or if you'd rather play it safe, just stick to ground transportation.

Boldly Go Where No Dead Person Has Gone Before
Use #82: Space Age Materials

Recreational space travel is still a distant fantasy for most people. When that day finally arrives the human body could provide some of the materials used for interplanetary day-tripping.

Beryllium is a strong, lightweight metal that maintains its integrity under extreme temperature conditions. These qualities make it ideal for space craft construction, such as the Saturn V rocket, in addition to instruments like the Spitzer and James Webb Space Telescopes. A human body isn't the best source for such a rare metal, though one dead human body does contain 36 micrograms.

A more abundant resource in a dead human body is oxygen, to the tune of 43 kilograms. Most of the oxygen in the human body is in the form of water, both of which are useful in space to fill oxygen tanks and provide sustenance to well-traveled astronauts.

Chapter 21
Outdoor Activities

"Once I realized how expensive funerals are, I began to exercise and watch my diet."

Thomas Sowell

A good way to avoid an early death is to maintain a regular exercise regimen, so it's ironic that the equipment for many outdoor activities could be fashioned from the remains of a dead human body.

Casketball
Use #83: Recreational Supplies

Are you ready to party like there's no tomorrow? You could swing by your local retail store and pick up some recreational supplies, or you could swing by your local morgue and pick up the materials to make your own supplies.

Indulge your passion for water sports by using these common materials found in the human body: the 43 kilograms of oxygen in one dead human body could fill 13 high-pressure steel oxygen tanks; a human skeleton also contains 120 mg of lead, enough of which could make a weight belt for scuba diving.

If you enjoy tennis, collect lots of dead human bodies and extract the 20 mg of titanium in each. Titanium is a sturdy material used for tennis rackets. If lacrosse suits your fancy, you'll need scores of dead human bodies to make a lacrosse stick out of scandium; each dead human body contains 0.2 mg. Tungsten dart tips are used in many indoor and outdoor activities. The scant 20 micrograms of tungsten in one dead human body will hardly be missed.

In fact, scour every graveyard in sight and collect enough tungsten to fashion a weight ballast for your yacht. Fishing sinkers could be crafted with the 0.5 mg of bismuth found in the human body, though you'll need a lot to make a sinker sufficient to catch a fish.

If the mounting death toll seems high for such

carefree excursions, consider staying home and take a dip in your swimming pool. And don't forget the chlorine: a 10-ounce chlorine tablet could be fashioned with the chlorine content of just three dead human bodies.

Finally, fireworks serve as the perfect nightcap after a long day of field sports, fishing and swimming. Luckily, you've already collected some valuable raw materials...

Crypt the Light Fantastic
Use #84: Fireworks

A fair amount of gunpowder could be mined from one dead human body (*see Use #43*). Gunpowder is the principle ingredient in fireworks, which explains why fireworks are so heavily regulated. In fact, fireworks rockets are similar to the rockets used by the military.

Gunpowder is fine for firecrackers, but a true fireworks display also demands bright colors, which are achieved by adding small amounts of certain chemicals. One dead human body contains rubidium, which is used to produce red and yellow fireworks. The strontium in one dead body could also produce red fireworks, while barium is used to produce blue and green fireworks and sodium produces yellow fireworks.

For added effect, charcoal can be added to a

fireworks rocket to produce a brilliant, blazing tail. As luck would have it, a dead human body can accommodate that, too…

B-B-Q You
Use #85: Charcoal

No picnic is complete without the flame-licked goodness of barbecued meat. Snooty food connoisseurs may quibble over the ideal fuel for a barbecue fire, but there's really only one choice for our picnic: charcoal briquettes.

Charcoal has been used as fuel for thousands of years. It's produced by burning a carbon-rich material, such as wood, to remove excess moisture and gas, making the resulting material slower-burning and nearly smokeless.

Modern charcoal briquettes contain additives that affect the cooking process and enhance a meal's flavor, but every type of charcoal contains carbon, as much as 98% of its total amount. The human body also contains a lot of carbon, equal to the carbon content of at least 36 pounds of charcoal.

Chapter 22
Vacation Destinations & Souvenirs

Being the only commuter on a train can be a lonely experience, unless you're dead. That's what a Croatian man discovered in 2007 when he boarded a night tram in Zagreb and passed away in his sleep. His dead body rode the tram for approximately six hours until the driver tried to wake his last remaining passenger at the end of the line.

Under different circumstances, a train ride can be an otherwise pleasant experience. Whatever mode of transportation you use, dead human bodies have played a central role in many vacation destinations and souvenirs.

How am I Going to Get This Through Customs?

Use #86: Keepsake Mummies

Napoleon Bonaparte, fresh from his successful military campaign against Austria in the 1790's, sought to strengthen his reputation as a strong leader by invading Egypt in 1798. He defeated the Mamluks, Egypt's military leadership, within months of landing on Egyptian soil, then launched a vast cultural expedition to study the country's rich culture. The *Institut de l'Égypte*, manned by 150 French scientists and scholars, was established in Cairo to collect, study and catalog thousands of years of Egyptian history.

Among the most important discoveries made by Napoleon's explorers was the Rosetta Stone, a giant stone slab containing a single passage written in three different languages, including the long-extinct Hieroglyphic language. Scholars were able to use the Rosetta Stone to translate the language of the pharaohs and unmask the mysteries of Ancient Egypt, ushering in a new, scientific age of Egyptology. If only the French had limited their curiosity to dead languages…

Among the artifacts collected, examined, and otherwise plundered by the French invaders were mummified human remains. Mummification was a common practice in Egypt for centuries, resulting in scores of bodies scattered across the country by the 1800's. French soldiers often collected the brittle, lightweight corpses while assisting scholars conducting surveys of historical sites and kept them as souvenirs.

The trend caught on. European noblemen throughout the 19th century made their own fashion statements by returning home at the conclusion of their Egyptian exploits with their own dead human body. Egyptian mummies were popular status symbols, often unveiled during cocktail parties, and likely helped a number of young men impress their sweethearts.

Most of the artifacts collected by the French, including the Rosetta Stone, were later claimed by the Brits and taken to England, where many are still on display in the British Museum. The mummies taken by the French are presumably still on display, too, and remain just as fashionable as the day they died.

Holy Bones
Use #87: Church of the Bones

Ossuary (noun)

--a place to deposit the bones of dead human bodies

The Sedlec Ossuary can be found in Kutna' Hora, a little town in the Czech Republic about 30 miles east of Prague. First constructed in 1132 AD, the ossuary gained fame in the 13th century when an abbot deposited a pocketful of dirt from Jerusalem in the local monastery's graveyard.

The holy soil made the site famous, especially when the black plague struck Europe and demand for burial plots skyrocketed. With thousands of dead bodies already buried in the graveyard, new human remains were stashed in the nearby All Saints Chapel. Endless piles of bones accumulated, and the chapel soon became an ossuary.

By 1870 the remains of over 40,000 dead human bodies resided in the ossuary, so the chapel's owner hired a local artisan, Frantisek Rint, to spruce up the place. His idea? Work with what you've got.

Rint used the thousands of human bones at his disposal to create decorative artwork. Femurs and hip bones adorn the many crucifixes and stone carvings within the structure. Stacks of human bones, some in the form of pyramids, can be found sequestered in different corners of the building. Perhaps most spectacular of all is the church's centerpiece, a giant chandelier layered with skulls and cross bones surrounded by spires topped with carved angels and skeletons. Rint even signed his work using human bones.

Curiosity seekers can preview the ossuary's awesome sight via the official website, http://www.kostnice.cz/. If you're fortunate enough to visit the Czech Republic, the Sedlec Ossuary is a mere ten minute walk from the central train station. The black death has long since passed, but the victims linger to tell the story.

Falling for the Lady
Use #88: Copper Plating

Since its completion in 1886, many daredevils, professional stunt men, and depressed souls have used the Statue of Liberty to take a flying leap into infamy.

In 1912 professional steeple climber Frederick R. Law was given permission to parachute from the observation deck located along the statue's torch. Law experienced difficulty deploying his parachute, resulting in a bumpy landing along the statue's grassy pedestal. He limped away, mostly unharmed.

89 years later, French stuntman Thierry Divaux (who goes by the nickname "Terry Do") was labeled an idiot by then-New York mayor Rudy Giuliani when Divaux parasailed onto the Statue of Liberty in an elaborate attempt to bungee jump from its torch. Alas, "Terry Do" got hung up while attempting to land and was found dangling off the statue until National Park and city police rescued him. Except for his ego, Divaux was otherwise uninjured.

The same cannot be said of Ralph Gleason, whose suicide was the first death to occur at the statue. On May 13, 1929, Gleason climbed out of one of the windows located along the statue's crown in an apparent attempt to kill himself. Witnesses reported seeing him back away from the ledge, possibly experiencing second thoughts, but instead Gleason lost his balance and fell backwards, hitting the statue's breast before free-falling to his death hundreds of feet below.

Dying at the foot of such an iconic symbol is a lousy way to make a name for yourself, so consider another way you can contribute to the statue's posterity. According to the National Park Service, the Statue of Liberty is plated with 62,000 pounds of copper. With a scant 72 mg per person, it would take over 390 million dead human bodies to provide enough copper to cover the entire statue. That's a lot of free-falls.

Chapter 23
Body Mining

"In this world nothing can be said to be certain, except death and taxes."

--Benjamin Franklin

A dead human body could net a tidy profit, considering the raw materials in the human body that could be used to make currency and other commodities.

Can You Spare Some Change?
Use #89: U.S. Coins

Have you ever found yourself digging around your pockets in search of loose change? Try digging a little deeper next time.

According to the United States Mint (usmint.gov), copper, zinc, manganese and nickel are the primary metals used to create U.S. coins. Each of these metals are also found in the human body.

Consider the much-maligned and often discarded penny. The Lincoln cent, first issued in 1909, was the first circulating U.S. coin to feature a real person, a former President of the United States. Released to commemorate the 100th anniversary of Abraham Lincoln's birth, it was initially made out of pure copper until the less expensive element zinc was added to the current copper-plated coin.

That's good for you, since the human body doesn't contain enough copper to make a pure, 2.5 gram Lincoln penny. But the human body does contain 2.3 grams of zinc, in addition to 72 milligrams of copper, which is almost the copper/zinc ratio found in a modern cent. Never mind a penny for your thoughts, for that price you could purchase the whole package. Congratulations, you're a real bargain.

Unfortunately, plumbing the human body for a nickel and dime's contents will require a higher body count. Copper and nickel are used to make five and ten-cent pieces, though the scant amount of nickel in the human body demands a contribution of 83 dead human bodies to make one five-cent piece, while a copper-rich dime requires the copper and nickel contributions of about 29 dead human bodies.

Quarters and half-dollars contain the same ratio of nickel and copper, though a half-dollar is exactly twice as big as a quarter. The combined contributions of 72 dead human bodies could manufacture one quarter; double that body count and you'll have yourself a half-dollar.

The rarely used, though highly collectible, Sacagawea (golden) dollar and presidential dollar coins are fashioned out of copper, nickel, zinc and manganese, which lends the coins their distinctive gold hue. Both coins are the exact same size and composition, and require the combined contributions of about 100 dead human bodies.

A dollar just doesn't buy what it used to, which hardly makes the sacrifice worth it, though it's a neat coincidence that one hundred dead human bodies could also produce 100 pennies, making the human body the perfect instrument for making change.

That'll Cost You an Arm and a Leg
Use #90: Human Organs on the Open Market

www.coolquiz.com was kind enough to crunch

the numbers on a variety of common elements found in the human body and estimate a market value for each, such as the iodine, fluorine and zinc that can be used for medical purposes. In addition, the 18 square feet of skin found on the human body, when valued according to the price of cowhide, all combine for a grand total of $4.50. Finally, a nest egg to retire on.

If moral ambiguity doesn't slow you down, a more lucrative market exists for your dead human body in the form of organ trafficking. Outlawed in most countries, human organ trafficking involves harvesting organs and body parts from living or recently deceased donors and selling the organs to the highest bidder. High demand, coupled with the low supply for usable, healthy donor organs, has led to exorbitant prices and criminal behavior.

Consider the fate of Alistair Cooke, world-famous host of the long-running television program *Masterpiece Theatre*. When Cooke passed away at the age of 95, his family made arrangements with a local crematorium to incinerate his body. Instead, the funeral director made arrangements with Michael Mastromarino, a former dental surgeon and owner of Biomedical Tissue Services who sawed into Cooke's disease-infested, cancer ridden body. He made off with $7,000 worth of bones before the desecrated remains were finally cremated and returned to Cooke's family.

Cooke's bones were deemed unsuitable for implantation, but Mastromarino made 4.6 million dollars over three years of illegal organ harvesting before authorities got wind of his activities and prosecuted him.

He and his associates later pled guilty to falsifying records and not checking whether the bodies of his victims carried infectious diseases.

Some countries allow the sale of human organs as a means of increasing supply, though most countries ban the process. Some organs, such as a single kidney, can be harvested from a living donor without causing death, but most cannot be procured until after the donor is deceased. If you don't mind cashing in until it's too late, your dead human body could make you, or at least your descendents, very rich.

Human Organ Facts

A living person selling his own kidney can net between $2,500-$3,000, while the organ broker can make as much as $100,000-$200,000.

A View to Make a Killing
Use #91: Gold Content

James Bond can fend off bad guys with a well-placed punch and a well-spoken pun, but the love interests in a *007* movie don't always live to see the end credits. Take Jill Masterson, who falls prey to an assassin (and lots of gold body paint) in the classic action film *Goldfinger*. Bond avenges his lover's death by foiling the title villain's attempt to plunder the gold supply stored within Fort Knox.

Goldfinger had his work cut out for him. The famed gold reserve is protected inside one of the most famous military bases in the world, located 35 miles south of Louisville, Kentucky. Over 57,000 people reside in and around the 110,000 acre base, including 23,000 soldiers, the 46th Infantry Regiment and the Eastern Region of the ROTC.

The U.S. Bullion Depository, which houses the gold reserve within Fort Knox, holds over 4,600 tons of gold, mostly in the form of 1,000-ounce gold bricks. The human body also holds a reserve of gold: a scant 0.2 milligrams. While a gold bar found in Fort Knox is valued at just over one million dollars (price per ounce based on the March 2008 market value of gold), the gold found in one dead human body is valued at just under one penny.

If a penny's worth of gold doesn't impress you, consider that the population of Fort Knox is worth $399 in gold. But that's chump change, since producing one pure-gold brick would require the contributions of 143,257,143 dead human bodies. That's a lot of bloodshed for 62.5 pounds of gold, though the dastardly Goldfinger would probably approve.

Olympic Bling-Bling
Use #92: Gold, Silver and Bronze Medals

The ancient Greek athletes who competed in the original Olympic Games didn't benefit from lucrative endorsement deals. But just like modern sports stars, those athletes were revered for their physical prowess and were rewarded with public adulation, plus an olive wreath placed on their heads during the closing ceremonies.

Today's Olympic winners can expect something pricier than a prickly bonnet--the iconic Olympic medal, which comes in three sporty colors: gold, silver and bronze. Since the modern Olympic Games were inaugurated in 1896, the size and composition of these medals have often changed. Recent games have awarded gold medals made mostly of silver; silver medals made of silver and lesser metals; and bronze medals made of bronze, pure copper, silver, zinc, or combinations of these metals and more.

One dead human body contains all of the elements used to make Olympic medals. The required amount of these elements has fluctuated with each game, though any Olympic medal would require the contributions of dozens, hundreds, sometimes thousands of dead human bodies.

Collecting that many donors would be a Herculean effort. If you're not an athlete but would like to contribute to the Olympic games, you could make a fashion statement by serving as the raw material for the world's greatest athletic award.

Olympic Facts

The first modern Olympians in Athens were awarded gold medals devoid of actual gold, instead composed of silver and copper, while silver medals were made entirely of copper.

The St. Louis Olympics of 1904 and the London games of 1908 were the first to use gold and silver for their respective medals, plus bronze, a copper/tin alloy, for the third place medal.

Chapter 24
Death is Taxing

Virgilio Cintron left his Manhattan apartment one Tuesday afternoon to cash his $355 social security check at a local Pay-O-Matic, just as he had many times before. The only difference this time was that he was dead.

You see, Virgilio's friends, David J. Dalaia and James O'Hare, loaded Virgilio's recently deceased body onto an office chair, wheeled him to the Pay-O-Matic, and parked his slumping body out front while they asked the clerk inside to cash his check. Not surprisingly, the police escorted the empty-handed pair away and wheeled Virgilio off to the morgue.

Where Dalaia and O'Hare failed, the indigenous people of Papua New Guinea and Zipangu, Japan succeeded by finding inventive, sometimes barbaric ways to use a dead human body as currency. Some people are worth more dead than alive. Just remember to leave the office chair, and other incriminating evidence, at home where they belong.

I'll Trade You This Femur For My Life
Use #93: Dead Body Trinkets

Deep in the South Pacific, along the borders of Australia and Indonesia, resides Papua New Guinea, a largely untouched island nation of over six million people and 900 languages. Europeans discovered the country shortly after Columbus landed in America, though it took centuries for the West to fully exploit its natural resources. Because they were overlooked for so many years, the natives of Papua New Guinea were able to bring many of their ancient traditions into the modern world.

The people of Vanatinai live in the southeastern tip of Papua New Guinea's Milne Bay province on an isolated island in the Louisiade Archipelago. Cut off from the mainland, the natives practice death rituals you'd be hard pressed to find at your neighborhood mortuary. The local government has tried to clamp down on these barbaric practices in recent years, but some traditions, like many of the things covered in this book, die hard.

Death among the people of Vanatinai is held in deep suspicion, often attributed to sorcery. Elaborate mourning rituals bring out members of surrounding tribes, allowing suspected sorcerers to clear their names by engaging in public bouts of weeping to demonstrate their sadness. Fear of death and those who cause it through the dark arts is so severe that the locals have developed methods to ward off evil spirits--and gain assistance from the spirit world--by using body parts taken from dead human bodies.

During the days and nights following a person's death, friends and family members will "speak" to the deceased and ask permission to take a *muramura*, a piece of the dead human's body. Teeth and hair are the most common body parts taken, though really intrepid tribe members will wait months after death to excavate the dead body and retrieve a jawbone, skull bone or anything else that tickles their funny bone.

This spiritual trinket is then used to negotiate with otherworldly spirits in a supernatural bartering ritual. The user may ask to have a disease cured, or something more benign like success in farming, commerce or romance. The body part can also be used as collateral to ask the deceased for ghostly assistance in the future, while really ambitious grave robbers will seek out old battlefields and dig up the bodies of fallen heroes who were celebrated for their success in war, love or business.

Body relics are cherished, but also feared for their magical power. Households containing a body relic are said to be "hot," or supernaturally hazardous, leading some owners to stash their body relic in a nearby forest. Owners who choose to carry it on their persons risk causing an uproar as old women and children may be driven to tears by its mere presence (understandable, considering it's a rotting body part taken under dubious circumstances).

Possessing a body relic is illegal under contemporary Papua New Guinea law as the government may suspect the owner of sorcery. The practice at the very least violates Papua New Guinea's burial regulations, which strive to maintain good hygienic practices throughout the island system. Of course, if someone is arrested under suspicion of sorcery, he could cash in his body relic and ask the spirit world to post his bail.

Who Do I Have to Kill to Beat This Murder Rap?
Use #94: Dead Body Retribution

The residents of Rossel Island, which neighbors Vanatinai in the Louisiade Archipelago of Papua New Guinea, share its fellow islander's suspicion of death--and penchant for bizarre mourning practices. The local government managed to curtail many disturbing traditions by the early 20th century, such as allowing a dead body to remain in the deceased's home for several months until the final stages of decomposition have left nothing but a collection of bones, which were then displayed on a mantelpiece. But despite government efforts, some bizarre burial rituals persist to this day.

The Yela, who reside on Rossel Island, are even-tempered people who usually avoid violent outbursts. A death in the family provides them with an occasion to express their concealed rage, even if the family member didn't die under unusual circumstances. Funeral services are held within a day or two after death, attended by family and other tribe members who live near enough to reach the event. Upon entering the dead person's home mourners surround the body and engage in tortured wailing, then move to a quiet corner of the house to mourn peacefully.

An old man from the village then officiates over a dialogue, which soon becomes an argument, over who is at fault. Family members (usually brothers, sons and nephews) hurl accusations at the attending mourners, engage in nasty threats and sometimes physical altercations. But this is just a prelude…the real bloodletting begins after the funeral.

Suspicion surrounding the death prompts accusations of sorcery. Tribe members accuse someone in a neighboring village of casting a spell on the deceased, then demand retribution from the accused sorcerer. Fearing revenge by angry family members, the accused "sorcerer" murders a member of his own village in a sacrificial ritual, then delivers the remains to the accusing family. This is believed to have once been a cannibalistic ceremony, which finds its modern incarnation in the form of an elaborate mortuary feast held after the funeral.

Killing a member of one's own tribe represented the most significant monetary payment in the Rossel Island economy, bestowing considerable prestige on the family that received the sacrifice. While it may seem contradictory for an accused murderer to commit murder in order to clear his name, the process no doubt discouraged anyone from engaging in actual witchcraft. With a funeral tradition like that, who needs sorcery anyway?

You'd Make a Tasty Meal
Use #95: Ransom Cannibalism

In addition to lending his name to a popular swimming pool game, Marco Polo was among the earliest European explorers to visit the Far East. His exploits traveling the Silk Road, a lucrative trade route between China and the Mediterranean Sea, and consorting with the powerful Mongol ruler Kublai Khan were detailed in his landmark autobiography *Il Milione* (*The Million*, or *The Travels of Marco Polo*). Polo's experiences seemed unbelievable to a skeptical public, including the monetary use he discovered for a human body in Japan.

Polo described a harsh punishment among the people of Zipangu, Japan, where prisoners were eaten if they could not raise enough money to pay their ransom. To offset the lost payment, the slain prisoner's body was prepared in a splendid feast served during a formal dinner ceremony. Complete with gourmet accoutrements, the feast was attended by the kidnapper's friends and family members. Whether true or a product of group-think, the human flesh was celebrated for its superior taste, a quality that satisfied the debt and no doubt encouraged future captives to pay their ransom.

Polo himself was nearly the main course in a cannibal feast. Forced to land his ship on the island of Sumatra, Polo took great pains to build trenches around his encampment to ward off local tribesmen, whom he suspected of possessing a voracious appetite for human flesh. To discourage their cravings, he initiated a bartering system with the natives and discovered that their diets were not exclusively cannibalistic when they accepted his offer to trade food.

It's not known who told Marco Polo of the Sumatran's eating habits, or whether the suspicion was grounded in fact. After he returned to Venice after a long voyage, his fellow countrymen dismissed, but were otherwise entertained, by Polo's wild narratives. Questions about Polo's authenticity continue to this day, but his popular autobiography entertained even his naysayers and fed the reading public's hunger for stories of primitive people eaters.

Chapter 25
Dead People in Literature

Police responding to a burst water pipe at a Long Island home in 2007 were shocked to discover the mummified remains of 70-year old Vincenzo Ricardo. Dead from natural causes and propped up in his chair, his home's low humidity had kept Ricardo's body preserved for about a year. Police couldn't explain why the man's unpaid power was still on after so many months, since he was found sitting in front of a blaring television set.

He should've picked up a good book instead.

Death waltzes through many literary works, arousing acts of revenge and bittersweet memories. Dead human bodies have also inspired political satire, tragic irony, and lots of scary stories, too. Anyone who says that literature is dead is gravely mistaken. It's not the books that are dead, just the subject matter.

I'll Have You for Dessert
Use #96: Titus Andronicus

Everyone knows that William Shakespeare was a great dramatist, but few people know that he was also an amateur chef. Consider this secret ingredient found in his play *Titus Andronicus*: two depraved brothers, strung up, tortured and their throats slit so that their blood may be baked into a pie.

Titus Andronicus is one of Shakespeare's bloodiest plays. The title character is a Roman general who starts a series of revenge killings that culminate in the rape and disfigurement of his only daughter, Lavinia. The perpetrators, Chiron and Demetrius, are the sons of Titus's enemy, Queen Tamora. Titus avenges his daughter's defilement by killing the two brothers and serving them to Queen Tamora under the guise of a reconciliation feast. Titus says of Chiron and Demetrius:

Why there they are, both baked in this pie,
Whereof their mother daintily hath fed,
Eating the flesh that she herself hath bred

But the fun doesn't end there. Titus kills his daughter as punishment for being raped (which kind of puts a damper on the whole vengeance thing), then kills Tamora before finally getting killed himself. You could say they all got their just desserts.

Nothing to Lose Your Head Over
Use #97: Hamlet

Hamlet, the title hero in Shakespeare's famous play, had a lot of emotional issues, not the least of which included his habit of talking to dead people.

You really can't blame the troubled kid. His mother married his uncle, the man who killed his father, the King. On top of that, Hamlet is told of this plot by his own dead father, who returns as a ghostly specter demanding that Hamlet avenge his murder.

So it's no wonder when Hamlet takes up residence in a graveyard and plucks a skull from the newly-dug ground. The skull belonged to Yorick, a jester who entertained Hamlet as a child. Hamlet says to his friend Horatio:

Alas, poor Yorick! I knew him, Horatio: a fellow of infinite jest, of most infinite fancy.

The skull reminds Hamlet of a better time in his life, when he was not plagued by thoughts of death and revenge. He describes the dead jester as an amusing man who bore the young Hamlet on his back during childhood games. But Yorick's current state invokes new feelings in Hamlet:

And now, how abhorred in my imagination it is..! Where be your gibes now? Your flashes of merriment, that were wont to set the table on a roar?

Yorick's skull represents Hamlet's bleak quest

for revenge, a quest instigated by murder--which will also end in murder. Hamlet also speculates on the current usefulness of the long-dead Alexander the Great:

Dost thou think Alexander looked o' this fashion i' the earth..? To what base uses we may return, Horatio! Why may not imagination trace the noble dust of Alexander, till he find it stuffing a bung-hole?

Hamlet concludes that one of history's greatest leaders has been reduced to cork used in a beer barrel. This dialogue furthers Hamlet's inner debate: if death is inevitable for all people, should he pursue his quest for revenge in light of the mounting death toll, or should he simply end his own misery by killing himself?

As fans of the play can attest, Hamlet's confusion ends in the deaths of many people, which could be viewed as poetic justice, bittersweet tragedy, or an excellent source for bottle stoppers. *To beer or not to beer...*

Baby Food
Use #98: A Modest Proposal

"I think it is agreed by all parties," begins Jonathan Swift's *A Modest Proposal*, "that this prodigious number of children in the arms, or on the backs, or at the heels of their mothers, and frequently of their fathers, is in the present deplorable state of the kingdom, a very great additional grievance." Swift was describing the state of the Irish people under British rule in 1729, particularly the young, underfed Irish children. Swift was being sarcastic when he wrote this passage, which was a relief considering his solution to the "grievance."

Swift published many pamphlets that challenged social injustice, in particular Britain's mistreatment of the Irish. *A Modest Proposal* is his most famous pamphlet because of its intense, brutal irony. Swift's words were over the top yet brutally felt for the people he described.

To drive home his point, Swift proposed a startling solution to end the Irish people's suffering: "I have been assured by a very knowing American of my acquaintance in London, that a young healthy child, well nursed, is at a year old, a most delicious, nourishing, and wholesome food; whether stewed, roasted, baked or boiled…." Lest the nature of this book has left any of you jaded, rest assured that cannibalizing young children was not a standard practice in 18th century England.

Swift suggested that eating Irish babies would relieve their poor parents of having to raise them, while also providing the British people with a cheap and tasty source of nourishment. Swift's rational argument defending such an inhuman practice amused his readers and highlighted the suffering caused by the British.

Swift might be the first writer in history to spin humor out of eating dead human babies, though satire in the modern world is a tool best used with a disclaimer: don't try this at home, unless the little babies have it coming.

The Unkindest Cut

Use #99: Sweeney Todd, The Demon Barber of Fleet Street

The Broadway musical *Sweeney Todd, The Demon Barber of Fleet Street* tells the story of a murderous barber who joins forces with an unscrupulous baker to dispose of his victims in the form of store-bought meat pies. Hard to believe, but some historical accounts claim the story of Sweeney Todd is based on fact.

The fictional Todd was a juvenile delinquent sent to prison in his mid-teens. After his release he sets up a barber shop in a crowded London district, where he proceeded to kill his customers and loot their bodies of clothing, money and wristwatches.

But murder is a messy business, and Todd soon found himself knee-deep in dead human bodies. So he enlists the help of a baker, Margery Lovett, and the wicked couple used the cut-up customers to whip up a meat pie recipe straight from hell, which did little to build Todd's reputation as a barber or inspire repeat business. Talk about biting the hand that feeds you.

Barber Facts

Barbers in the 18th century did more than cut hair. They also treated the sick and even performed minor surgical procedures like bloodletting and teeth-pulling.

Waking Up the Dead
Use #100: Frankenstein

Movie fans will be disappointed to learn that electricity played no part in resurrecting "the creature" in Mary Shelley's original novel *Frankenstein*. Despite the lightning rods, neck bolts, and electric eels featured in some of the story's many film incarnations, Shelley's creation simply comes to life after its parts have been sewn together. The real shock comes later.

Nor was a criminal's mind implanted in the creature's head, as dramatized in several movie versions. Shelley's creation was born with a blank slate. It learned evil by watching how humanity reacted to its hideous appearance. The creature commits several murders after its horrified creator, Viktor Frankenstein, rejects the creature after its "birth," leading to a cat and mouse chase through the arctic wilderness.

The creature threatens to take more lives unless Viktor builds it a mate. Not wanting to make the same mistake twice, Victor aborts his plans to construct a mate and chases the creature deep into the north pole where both are fated to perish. Robbed of his loved ones and crippled by the guilt of his ambitions, Viktor discovers that creating life, especially with materials taken from dead human bodies, can only lead to a dead end.

Epilogue
Book of the Dead

Use #101: Bookmaking

"I lived to write and wrote to live."

--Samuel Rogers, English Poet

Many writers hope to attain immortality through their work. Sadly, most never achieve their goal…at least not with words, anyway, but how about in the form of actual pen and paper? Could a dead human body provide the raw materials to print a book?

As we learned with Uses #49 and #69, properly treated human skin could serve as clothing fabric, furniture upholstery, or sailing material. Human leather could also be used to make a book cover, while leather paper is used in arts & crafts, stationary, and even printing. Additionally, the average human skeleton weighs about 30 pounds, which would've come in handy in Ancient China where oracles wrote prophecies on animal bones.

Uses #61 and #62 discussed how pencil lead and photocopier ink could be produced from the 35 pounds of carbon in one dead human body. The average person also contains five quarts of blood; bestselling author Stephen King is fabled to have once ended a lengthy book signing by writing his signature using his cracked, bloody fingers.

So there you have it. It may not be the prettiest-looking book, and OSHA may slap it with a hazardous waste disclaimer, but one dead human body does contain the raw materials needed to produce a manuscript. Everyone thinks they have a book in them. Turns out they're right.

Appendix

101 Dead Body Trivia Questions

(Answers found at the bottom of each page)

I. Match the reputed last words with the performing artist who spoke them.

1) "I should never have switched from Scotch to Martinis."
2) "I've had a hell of a lot of fun and I've enjoyed every minute of it."
3) "That guy's gotta stop…he'll see us"
4) "That was a great game of golf, fellers."
5) "This is it. I'm going. I'm going."

a) James Dean
b) Bing Crosby
c) Al Jolson
d) Errol Flynn
e) Humphrey Bogart

1) e 2) d 3) a 4) b 5) c

II. Which of these actors/actresses did *not* die in a road accident?

6)
a) James Dean
b) Desmond Llewelyn ("Q" from the James Bond films)
c) Montgomery Clift
d) All of them died in road accidents
e) None of them died in a road accident

7)
a) Grace Kelly
b) Vivien Leigh
c) Jayne Mansfield
d) All of them died in road accidents
e) None of them died in a road accident

6) c 7) b

III. Match the tombstone epitaphs with the correct actor/actress.

8) We live to love you more each day
9) She did it the hard way
10) That's all folks!
11) I never met a man I didn't like
12) Beloved Father

a) Mel Blanc
b) Jayne Mansfield
c) Bela Lugosi
d) Bette Davis
e) Will Rogers

8) b 9) d 10) a 11) e 12) c

IV. Human Body Nutrients

13) One dead human body contains the calcium content of ___ half-cup servings of kelp.

a) Two b) 15 c) 165

14) One dead human body contains the iron content of ___ *Marie Callender's* Beef Stroganoff and Noodles w/Carrots and Peas dinners.

a) 78 b) 512 c) 2029

15) One dead human body contains the phosphorus content of ___ cups of orange juice.

a) over 850 b) over 1,850 c) over 18,500

16) One dead human body contains the potassium content of ___ servings of baked potato.

a) 244 b) 24,400 c) over 2 million

17) One dead human body contains the sodium content of ___ 10-ounce bags of *Fritos* chips.

a) 17 b) 91 c) 265

18) One dead human body contains the zinc content of ___ raw oyster(s).

a) one b) 13 c) 277

13) b 14) c 15) c 16) a 17) b 18) c

V. Match the song titles with the correct recording artist.

19) *Thing to Do In Denver When You're Dead*

20) *Wanted Dead or Alive*

21) *Living Dead Girl*

22) *Dead Girls of London*

23) *Deadbeat Holiday*

a) Frank Zappa

b) Green Day

c) Warren Zevon

d) Bon Jovi

e) Rob Zombie

19) c 20) d 21) e 22) a 23) b

VI. Which of these musical performers did *not* die in a road accident?

24)
a) Duane Allman
b) Lisa Lopes
c) Dottie West
d) All of them died in road accidents
e) None of them died in a road accident

25)
a) Glenn Miller
b) Janis Joplin
c) Otis Redding
d) All of them died in road accidents
e) None of them died in a road accident

24) d   25) e

VII. Match the tombstone epitaphs with the correct musical performers.

26)
The best is yet to come

27)
Everybody loves somebody sometime

28)
Thank you for all the love you gave me.
There could be no one stronger.
Thank you for the many beautiful songs.
They will live long and longer

29)
The Entertainer
He did it all

30)
A star on earth - a star in heaven

a) Karen Carpenter
b) Frank Sinatra
c) Sammy Davis, Jr.
d) Dean Martin
e) Hank Williams

26) b 27) d 28) e 29) c 30) a

VIII. Which of these recording artists did *not* die in a plane crash?

31)
a) Warren Zevon
b) John Denver
c) Jim Croce
d) All of them died in plane crashes
e) None of them died in plane crashes

32)
a) Buddy Holly
b) Ricky Nelson
c) Roy Orbison
d) All of them died in plane crashes
e) None of them died in plane crashes

33) Which recording artist wrote the lyric, "It's better to burn out than to fade away?"

a) Jimi Hendrix
b) Jim Morrison
c) Neil Young

31) a 32) c 33) c

IX. Elements in the human body

34) The cadmium in one dead human body could ______.

a) fit on the head of a pin
b) fashion a paper weight
c) fill a cannonball

35) The potassium in one dead human body could ______.

a) fit on the head of a pin
b) fashion a paper weight
c) fill a cannonball

36) The aluminum in one dead human body could ______.

a) fit on the head of a pin
b) fashion a paper weight
c) fill a cannonball

37) The carbon in one dead human body could ______.

a) fit on the head of a pin
b) fashion a paper weight
c) fill a cannonball

38) The sulfur in one dead human body could ______.

a) fit on the head of the pin
b) fashion a paper weight
c) fill a cannonball

34) a 35) b 36) a 37) c 38) b

X. Match the reputed last words with the writer who spoke them.

39)
"Goodnight my darlings, I'll see you tomorrow."

40)
"Turn up the lights, I don't want to go home in the dark."

41)
"I've had 18 straight whiskeys. I think that's a record."

42)
"God bless…God damn."

43)
"This is no time to make new enemies."

a) Dylan Thomas
b) Voltaire
c) O. Henry
d) Noel Coward
e) James Thurber

39) d 40) c 41) a 42) e 43) b

XI. Which of the following writers did *not* commit suicide?

44)
a) Mary Shelley
b) Bram Stoker
c) H.G. Wells
d) All of them committed suicide
e) None of them committed suicide

45)
a) Virginia Woolf
b) F. Scott Fitzgerald
c) Ernest Hemingway
d) All of them committed suicide
e) None of them committed suicide

46) Which poet wrote the following verse:

Because I could not stop for Death
He kindly stopped for me
The carriage held but just Ourselves
And Immortality

a) Emily Dickinson
b) Ralph Waldo Emerson
c) Edgar Allan Poe

44) e 45) b 46) a

XII. Match the tombstone epitaphs with the correct writers.

47)
I had a lover's quarrel with the world.

48)
The Stone the Builders Rejected

49)
And alien tears will fill for him
Pity's long broken urn,
For his mourners will be outcast men,
And outcasts always mourn.

50)
Against you I will fling myself
Unvanquished and unyielding, O Death!

51)
Don't Try

a) Virginal Woolf
b) Jack London
c) Robert Frost
d) Charles Bukowski
e) Oscar Wilde

47) c 48) b 49) e 50) a 51) d

XIII. Match the plot with the Stephen King story:

52)
A husband dies while his wife is handcuffed to their bed.

53)
An innkeeper is haunted by ghosts that drive him insane.

54)
A doctor uses an ancient Indian burial ground to resurrect his dead son.

55)
Four friends hit the road in search of a missing boy who is presumed dead.

56)
A prison inmate has the power to heal the terminally ill.

57)
A small New England town is besieged by a vampire.

a) *Pet Sematary*
b) "The Body"
c) *The Green Mile*
d) *Gerald's Game*
e) *Salem's Lot*
f) *The Shining*

52) d 53) f 54) a 55) b 56) c 57) e

XIV. Human Pelts

58) How many wallets could be fashioned from the tanned skin of one dead human body?

a) 10
b) 40
c) 80

59) How many passport holders could be fashioned from the tanned skin of one dead human body?

a) 12
b) 32
c) 52

60) How many small brief cases could be fashioned from the tanned skin of one dead human body?

a) 4
b) 14
c) 24

58) b 59) b 60) a

XV. Match the reputed last words with the world leader who spoke them.

61)
"Why are you weeping? Did you imagine that I was immortal?"

62)
"Farewell, my children, forever. I go to your father."

63)
"Josephine…"

64)
"Shoot me in the chest!"

65)
"Go on, get out-last words are for fools who haven't said enough."

a) Karl Marx
b) Napoleon I
c) Benito Mussolini
d) Marie Antoinette
e) Louis XIV

61) e 62) d 63) b 64) c 65) a

XVI. World History

66) Approximately how many Egyptians were mummified during the 3,000 years the technique was practiced in Egypt?

a) 700,000
b) 7 million
c) 70 million

67) The tomb of which Egyptian ruler was discovered in 1922, launching worldwide interest in Ancient Egyptian history?

a) Tutankhamen
b) Cleopatra
c) Nefertiti

68) The 5,300-year old mummified corpse found in the Italian Alps in 1991 was nicknamed:

a) Björn the Iceman
b) Ötzi the Iceman
c) Börje the Iceman

69) A Russian museum of erotica claims to own the 11-inch castrated member of this famed Czarist adviser, which is fabled to have fertility powers.

a) Yuri Zhivago
b) Grigori Rasputin
c) Dr. Strangelove

66) c 67) a 68) b 69) b

XVII. Match the tombstone epitaphs with the correct historical figures.

70)
Liberty, Humanity, Justice, Equality.

71)
A tomb now suffices him for whom the world was not enough

72)
Free at last. Free at last. Thank God almighty, I'm free at last.

73)
Workers of all lands unite. The philosophers have only interpreted the world in various ways; the point however is to change it.

a) Alexander the Great
b) Martin Luther King, Jr.
c) Susan B. Anthony
d) Karl Marx

70) c 71) a 72) b 73) d

XVIII. Match the reputed last words with the U.S. President who spoke them.

74)
"Is it the Fourth?"

75)
"Put out the light."

76)
"I have a terrific headache."

77)
"It is well, I die hard, but I am not afraid to go."

78)
"Thomas Jefferson survives…"

a) Franklin D. Roosevelt
b) John Adams
c) George Washington
d) Thomas Jefferson
e) Theodore Roosevelt

74) d 75) e 76) a 77) c 78) b

XIX. American Presidents

79) Which U.S. President said: "Mankind must put an end to war, or war will put an end to mankind?"

a) Abraham Lincoln
b) Franklin D. Roosevelt
c) John F. Kennedy

80) Which two founding fathers died on the same day, July 4th, 1826?

a) George Washington and Thomas Jefferson
b) Thomas Jefferson and Benjamin Franklin
c) Benjamin Franklin and George Washington
d) John Adams and Thomas Jefferson
e) George Washington and John Adams

81) A 2007 book by Thomas J. Craughwell details a plot to steal which U.S. President's dead body?

a) Andrew Jackson
b) Abraham Lincoln
c) Ulysses S. Grant

82) How many U.S. Presidents have been assassinated?

a) two
b) three
c) four

79) c 80) d 81) b
82) c (Lincoln, Garfield, McKinley, Kennedy)

XX. Match the tombstone epitaphs with the correct famous Americans.

83)
Author of the Declaration of American Independence
Of the Statute of Virginia for Religious Freedom
And Father of the University of Virginia

84)
Within this enclosure rest the remains of Gen. _________.

85)
At Rest
An American Soldier
And Defender of the Constitution

a) Jefferson Davis
b) George Washington
c) Thomas Jefferson

83) c 84) b 85) a

86)
Which famous American had once hoped his epitaph would read, "The body of ________, printer, like the cover of an old book, its contents worn out, and stript of its lettering and gilding, lies here, food for worms. Yet the work shall not be wholly lost, for it will, as he believed, appear once more in a new and more beautiful edition, corrected and amended by the Author?"

a) Thomas Edison
b) Benjamin Franklin
c) Mark Twain

86) b

XXI. Match the plot with the correct George A. Romero horror film.

87)
Flesh-eating zombies attack a group of people in a shopping mall.

88)
Flesh-eating zombies attack a group of people making a movie.

89)
Flesh-eating zombies attack a group of people in an underground bunker.

90)
Flesh-eating zombies attack a group of people in a farmhouse.

91)
Flesh-eating zombies attack a group of people in a fortified city.

a) Night of the Living Dead
b) Land of the Dead
c) Diary of the Dead
d) Dawn of the Dead
e) Day of the Dead

87) d 88) c 89) e 90) a 91) b

XXII. Film & Television

92) A 1962 episode of *The Twilight Zone* depicted aliens who harvest humans for food. What was the name of the cookbook that exposed their plan?

a) People Portions
b) To Serve Man
c) 101 Ways to Cook a Dead Human Body

93) Name the Charlton Heston film in which dead human bodies are used to manufacture food.

a) The Omega Man
b) The Last Hard Men
c) Soylent Green

94) How many times did Bela Lugosi play Count Dracula in a feature-length film?

a) two b) seven c) 12

95) How many times did Boris Karloff play Frankenstein's creature in a feature-length film?

a) one b) two c) three

96) Which one of these horror icons was buried in his famous creature costume?

a) Bela Lugosi (Dracula)
b) Boris Karloff (Frankenstein's creature)
c) Lon Chaney Jr. (The Wolf Man)

92) b 93) c 94) a 95) c 96) a

XXIII. Dead Body Potpourri

97) Which one of these pop culture luminaries did *not* die in a road accident?

a) Sam Kinison
b) Jackson Pollock
c) Calvert DeForest (Larry "Bud" Melman)
d) All of them died in road accidents
e) None of them died in road accidents

98) Which one of these athletes did *not* die in a plane crash?

a) Roberto Clemente
b) Rocky Marciano
c) Knute Rockne
d) All of them died in plane crashes
e) None of them died in plane crashes

99) Which philosopher said, "An unexamined life is not worth living?"

a) Socrates b) Aristotle c) Plato

100) True or false: Walt Disney's dead body is cryogenically frozen?

a) true b) false

101) Which comedian said: "It's not that I'm afraid to die. I just don't want to be there when it happens?"

a) Woody Allen b) George Carlin
c) Jerry Seinfeld

97) c 98) d 99) a 100) b 101) a

Answer Key

I. 1) e, 2) d, 3) a, 4) b, 5) c.

II. 6) c, 7) b

III. 8) b, 9) d, 10) a, 11) e, 12) c

IV. 13) b, 14) c, 15) c, 16) a, 17) b, 18, c

V. 19) c, 20) d, 21) e, 22) a, 23) b

VI. 24) d, 25) e

VII. 26) b, 27) d, 28) e, 29) c, 30) a

VIII. 31) a, 32) c, 33) c

IX. 34) a, 35) b, 36) a, 37) c, 38) b

X. 39) d, 40) c, 41) a, 42) e, 43) b

XI. 44) e, 45) b, 46) a

XII. 47) c, 48) b, 49) e, 50) a, 51) d

XIII. 52) d, 53) f, 54) a, 55) b, 56) c, 57) e

XIV. 58) b, 59) b, 60) a

XV. 61) e, 62) d, 63) b, 64) c, 65) a

XVI. 66) c, 67) a, 68) b, 69) b

XVII. 70) c, 71) a, 72) b, 73) d

XVIII. 74) d, 75) e, 76) a, 77) c, 78) b

XIX. 79) c, 80) d, 81) b, 82 c

XX. 83) c, 84) b, 85) a, 86) b

XXI. 87) d, 88) c, 89) e, 90) a, 91) b

XXII. 92) b, 93) c, 94) a, 95) c, 96) a

XXIII. 97) c, 98) d, 99) a, 100) b, 101) a

For more information about *Grave Anatomy*, visit

http://graveanatomy.com/.

For more information about Alex Reece, visit

http://www.alexreeceart.com/.

www.ingramcontent.com/pod-product-compliance
Lightning Source LLC
Chambersburg PA
CBHW050113280326
41933CB00010B/1086

* 9 7 8 0 9 9 1 2 8 4 5 3 5 *